The Poetics

Lucy Ives
Matthew Connors

The Poetics

Image Text Ithaca Press

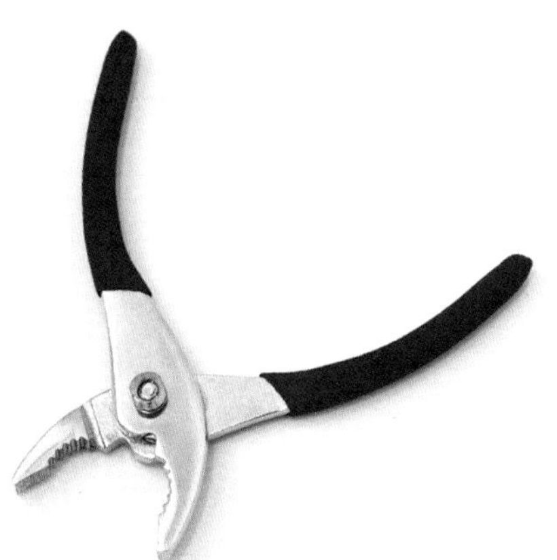

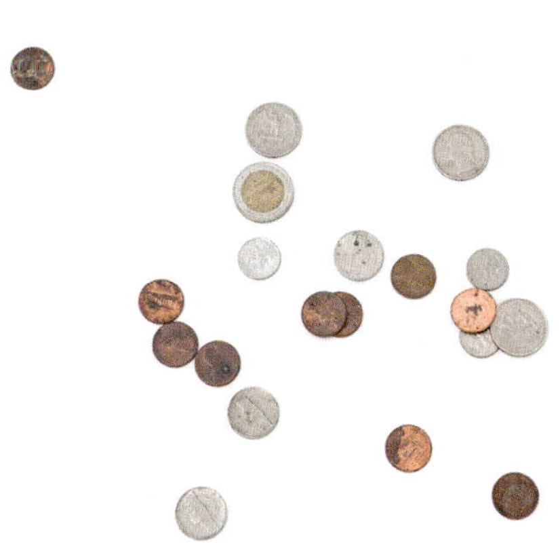

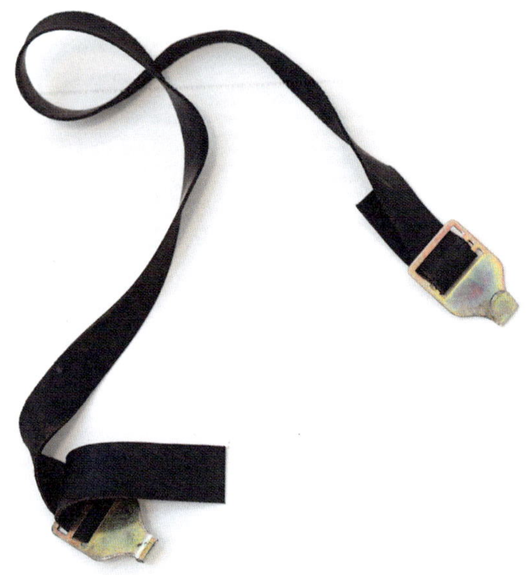

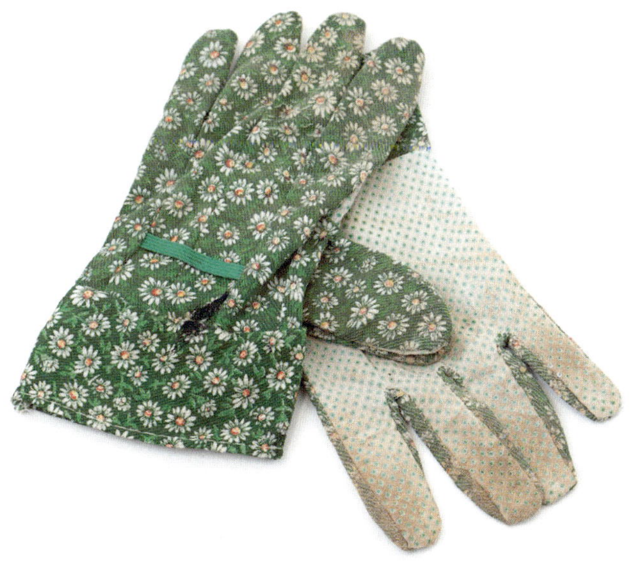

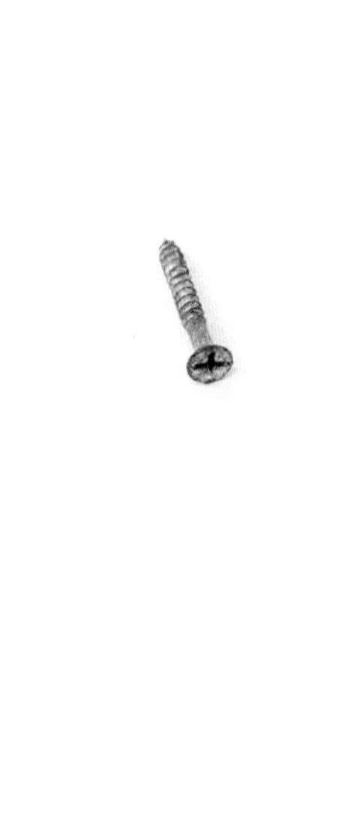

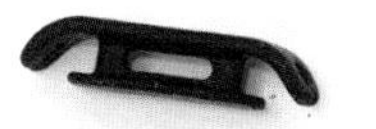

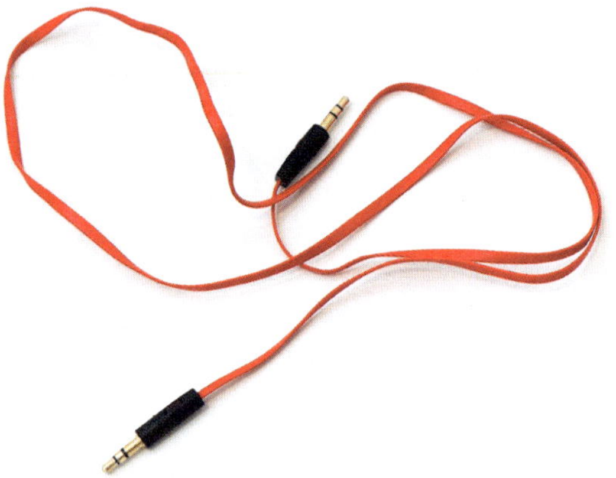

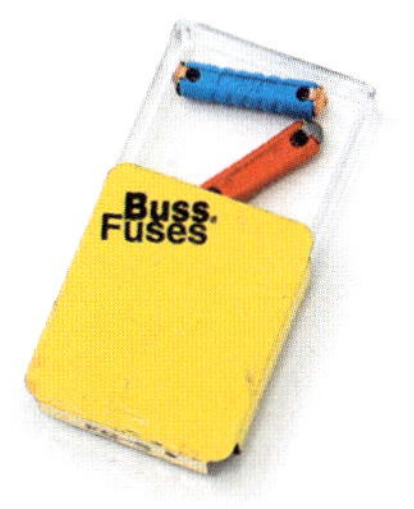
Buss
Fuses

I.

We are ever at the ready to construct objects in certain ways, conceptually speaking: as objects of a certain story, as tools in a given kind of narrative work. We believe we know where they begin—and where they end.

Also, there aren't really any secrets in this world. But there are kinds of information about history that we are not, strictly speaking, supposed to have. It has long been my goal to think about these kinds of information.

To put this a little differently, I wonder: How can poetic, fictional, or experimental—literary—modes give us new ways of reading and writing history?

I am not, by the way, interested in writing as a mode of proof or evidence. I am interested in it precisely for what it cannot prove, for what it may show as not the case, as excluded or merely possible.

What is the quality of the time in which we now live? It might be easy to judge it by its dominant modes, to term it a bureaucratic time that is rapidly becoming an all-but-entirely technocratic time. And, in greater detail, a stylized hierarchy in which future is classed above past and present, with present time viewed as either an obstacle or resource, something to be "gotten through" or "made the most of," while the past remains a treasured myth or otherwise vast and often unavailable quantity masked by traumatic dislocation.

Yet, we also know the present as an allegedly plentiful, multifarious extent, i.e., lifestyle. Time takes on qualities based on objects and milieus, particularly via entities that demand our attention, media, texts, platforms, programs—and so forth. There are various kinds of times, rather than a single time, within the contemporary era. There is never enough of them, of it.

An asymmetry remains: If there are so many presents, there must be as many pasts, must have been. In spite of this, we seem confident in thinking of a monolithic Past, something as universal as the present is personal and distinct. We must all contend, live with, break with the past, or so we like to say. And while it is easy to claim that everyone has a unique perspective on the present, it is more difficult to make an analogous contention with respect to what has come before.

This might remain a matter for the mutterings of common sense, were it not so strange a paradox of historical time, that as a writer I might be called upon to construct my own authority in relation to something I have not, and cannot have, experienced. Indeed, the paradox is only further enhanced by commonplace notions of the subject of history, who will seldom have been cognizant of the fact that she was present at or undergoing an event of history, much less that she underwent any event, so called. Placed firmly in the continuity and plenitude of present occurrence, she may become a subject of history experiencing its ineluctable material and pragmatic truth, even or especially *on account of* her own agnosticism with respect to an experience's discrete limits or cultural meaning. I, as researcher, value her because she knows more about a given moment of the past than I ever will, precisely because she is ignorant of what I was always going to come to know, i.e., what the passage of a certain amount of time, plus her agency within it, would, must, inevitably come to mean within a particular historical, narrative sequence. In this scenario, comprehending the meaning of a given event would seem to *preclude* experiencing it. These distinctions only serve to emphasize the potentially foolish and artificial nature of historical sequence and narrative time, with respect to research. And yet: Who can claim to have written a historical account without making use of them?

I say any of these things because of what I have lately come to perceive with regard to the present, which seems to me to be so oddly and distinctly composed of disparate, heterogeneous moments, temporalities, paces, perceptions, and subjects—some pressed into service of something called the contemporary, which is itself so wildly heterotopic as to defy categorization, even in the age of Google, Facebook, [*insert data-harvester du jour here*].

Often it is our sense that attention is so poorly or unevenly meted out that we remain unaware of our actual relation to the unfolding "now," as much as to the eons of past time, some of which we may have lived through but most of which are entirely barred from our phenomenal consciousness except via various records, archives, images, mediating traces. We could speak of history's present constitution through economies of attention, now that we are inundated with parseable data. Which data will we choose to read, to incorporate? How will the data we choose garner immanence, which is to say, plausibility? And, perhaps most importantly, given the wildly heterogeneous nature of present time, how can we restore to the past some of its own former heterogeneity? How can we grant it the discontinuity it once held, as a present, or series of presents, inhabited by a vast plurality of subjects, materials, languages, etc.? Could anyone ever hope to write such a narrative? Indeed, would it even be narrative?

In one of the great novels discussing the terrifying discontinuity of historical experience, 1925's *Mrs. Dalloway*, Virginia Woolf creates a character who has gone to war and who can no longer participate in the linguistic group to which he had formerly belonged. Like Hugo von Hofmannsthal's "Lord Chandos," another chronologically displaced literary figure, Septimus cannot stop sensing time in its particulars as cultural-linguistic concept, as the shards of science/technology, rather than as an inhabitable, familiar present. In one of the most beautiful passages in all of twentieth-century literature, Virginia Woolf describes this discursive isolation and displacement:

> He had only to open his eyes; but a weight was on them; a fear. He strained; he pushed; he looked; he saw Regent's Park before him. Long streamers of sunlight fawned at his feet. The trees waved, brandished. We welcome, the world seemed to say. And as if to prove it (scientifically) wherever he looked, at the houses, at the railings, at the antelopes stretching over the palings, beauty sprang instantly. To watch a leaf quivering in the rush of air was an exquisite joy. Up in the sky swallows swooping, swerving, flinging themselves in and out, round and round, yet always with perfect control as if elastics held them; and the flies rising and falling; and the sun spotting now this leaf, now that, in mockery, dazzling it with soft gold in pure good temper; and now and again some chime (it might be a motor horn) tinkling divinely on the grass stalks—all of this, calm and reasonable as it was, made out of ordinary things as it was, was the truth now; beauty, that was the truth now. Beauty was everywhere.

"It is time," said Rezia.

The word "time" split its husk; poured its riches over him; and from his lips fell like shells, like shavings from a plane, without his making them, hard, white, imperishable, words, and few to attach themselves to their places in an ode to Time. He sang. Evans answered from behind the tree. The dead were in Thessaly, Evans sang, among the orchids.

Septimus reminds me of a contemporary reader. Or, his sensations as described by Woolf remind me of the way in which reading is distributed in our present—as practice/action/media/instrumental time: a weird object as impossibly thick as it is impossibly piece-y, fugitive, brittle. I'm reminded of this by Septimus's "imperishable," chemical words.

The critic and scholar Sara Ahmed has a different line of interpretation, only loosely related to my own but quite relevant to what I am attempting to think about here. Writing on Woolf's novel in an essay about happiness and difference, she sees Septimus's suffering, a suffering caused by past events, not as contagious, per se, but as significantly effecting, world-making, even. Septimus and the novel's title character, a wealthy woman whose individuality has been largely erased by marriage, only pass each other by on the street. Ahmed writes:

> They do not catch sadness from each other; their sadness is what keeps alive histories that are not shared, that cannot be shared, as they pass by on the street. And yet something is shared, perhaps those very things that cannot simply be revealed.

The reader of *Mrs. Dalloway* understands the meaningful coincidence of the physical proximity of the novel's protagonist to the passing young man who will later take his own life and become an anecdote at her party. Mrs. Dalloway, however, does not recognize Septimus as an acquaintance or ally of any kind. The story of his death seems merely to interrupt her thoughts during the course of her carefully arranged festivities. Ahmed argues that what is in fact diverting Clarissa Dalloway's thoughts is not Septimus's death—at least, not solely. What is interrupting her social reverie is the meeting of her own unhappiness with that of another, in that of another, *as*. Clarissa Dalloway's own suffering comes home to her, for a moment, bearing another's name, to teach her about her "own resistances to recognizing those seemingly 'little' uneasy feelings of loss or dissatisfaction as unhappiness with [her own] life as such."

In other words, Clarissa cannot get into the time, the events that have been lived by Septimus, to live them, too. But she cannot escape them, either.

We feel ourselves displaced, reduced, managed by various temporalities and kinds of mediation—the unevenness of reading in print as opposed to online, and then the variously organized distraction and (sometimes painful) absorption that is reading on the Web. The present obsesses us, but we could also long to rediscover the past's own mediated heterogeneity. Some preliminary observations:

A. A feeling of a mixture of temporalities is a primary characteristic of present time.

B. Yet we behave "so" historically, even as the present presents us with an uneven temporal extent. We are already speaking about an orderly narrative, as, and again, this is common sense, history is "taking place" around us, with bizarre diversity.

C. What is research now, in an era of apparently infinite storage?

In scholarly histories, there would seem to be no place for the plausible, the nearly actual, as opposed to the measured, the studied, the true. But is it not also the case that the scholarly text suffers for its decorous refusal of the fictive? Could, at any rate, a history engage fiction without itself becoming incorrect, untrue, or otherwise worthless? Could there be any use in taking such an antithetical status on?

You think that narrative turns around lines, but it doesn't. In fact, it turns around glances. Narrative is not a through-line but rather a relay. Even when a single narrator speaks—and only of herself—she must make use of various reflective surfaces.

I want to advise a testing of the limits of critical time.

A trusted reader recently wrote to me:

> I found myself asking small questions in the margins as I read. These questions weren't terribly sophisticated. Usually, they were along the lines of: "what does this have to do with that?" or "could this thought be clearer?" (Surely this is a product of reading too much of the formulaic, cause-and-effect driven fiction that we talked about.) And then, once I finished reading the story, I went back to look at these questions and deleted each one of them. I deleted them because I'd realized that they weren't supposed to have answers, that they couldn't have answers. Our lives are defined by the breaking down (or outright lack) of narrative cohesion between events. That produces an existential confusion that is undeniable and worth exploring in art but rarely plumbed in short fiction. It's more easily produced in the spaces that poetry allows, or in visual art. There's confusion in this story, but it's a productive and, I think, beautiful confusion. While possible connections emerge as feelings, it's not entirely clear how the events of the story lead to, or can be traced back to, other events in the story. Instead, the events mingle together in a way that feels vital and undeniably true. Rather than solve the inherent confusion, the story arrives at a truth about the confusion itself: that beneath it, there is something else. An endlessness, perhaps, or the realization that we cannot know if an event is an origin or a conclusion, and that therein lies a kind of harmony.

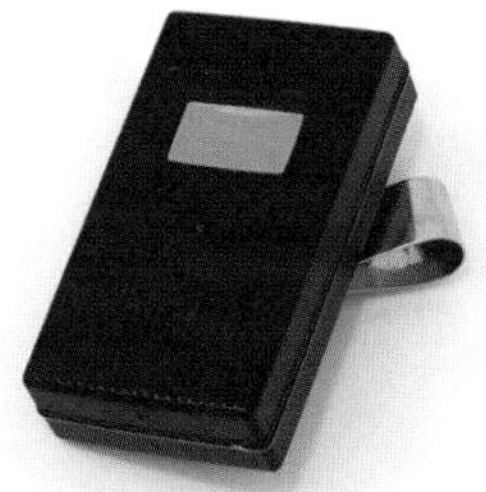

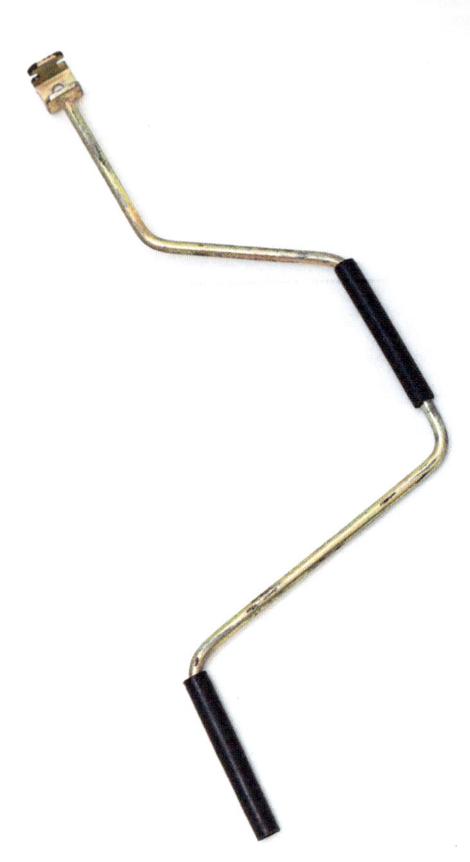

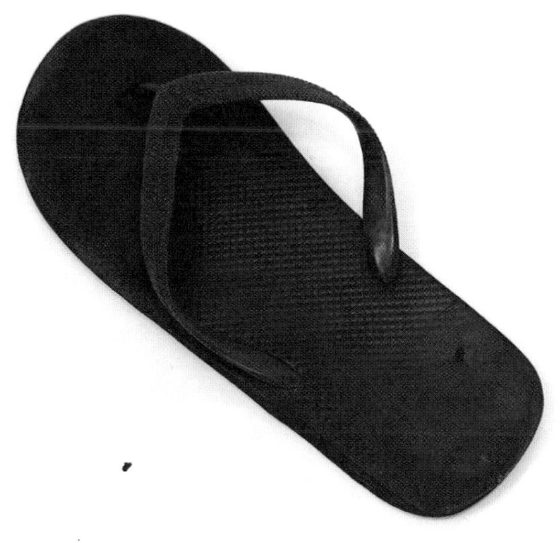

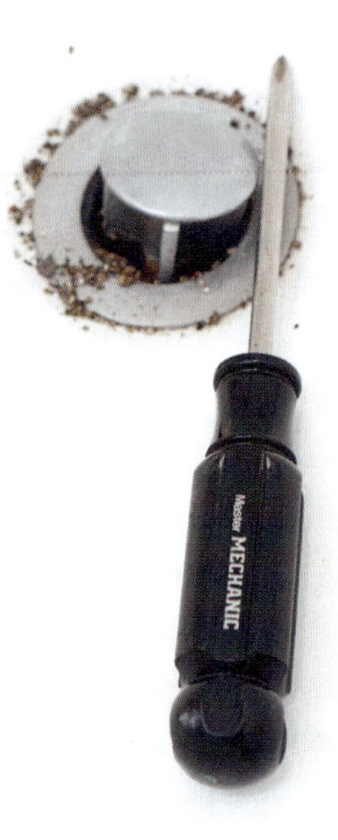
Master MECHANIC

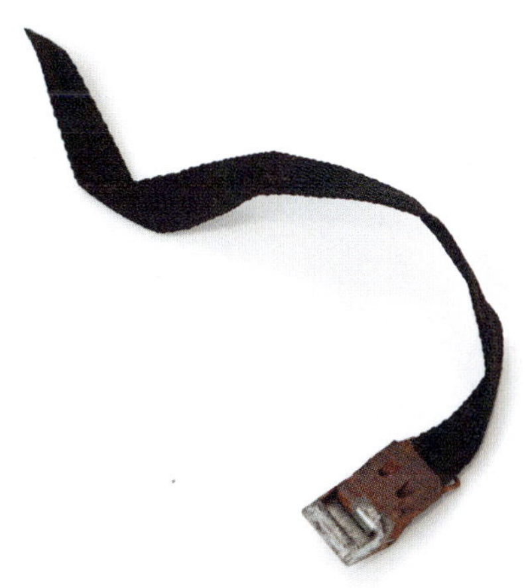

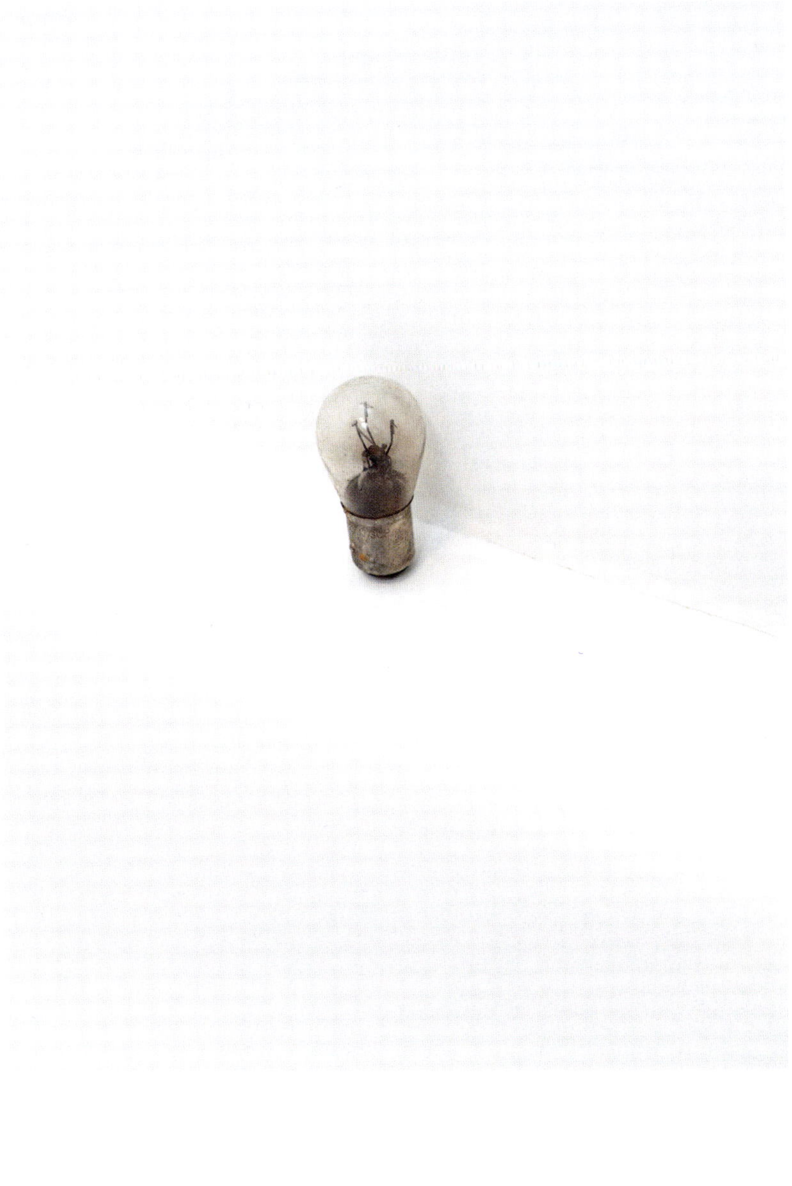

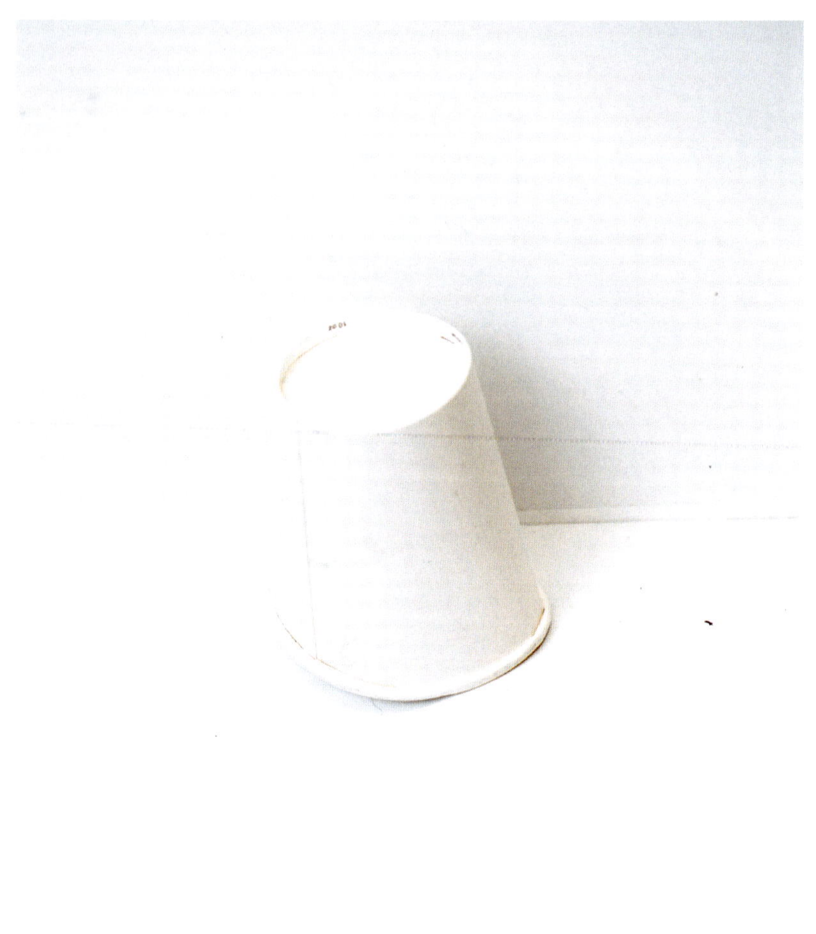

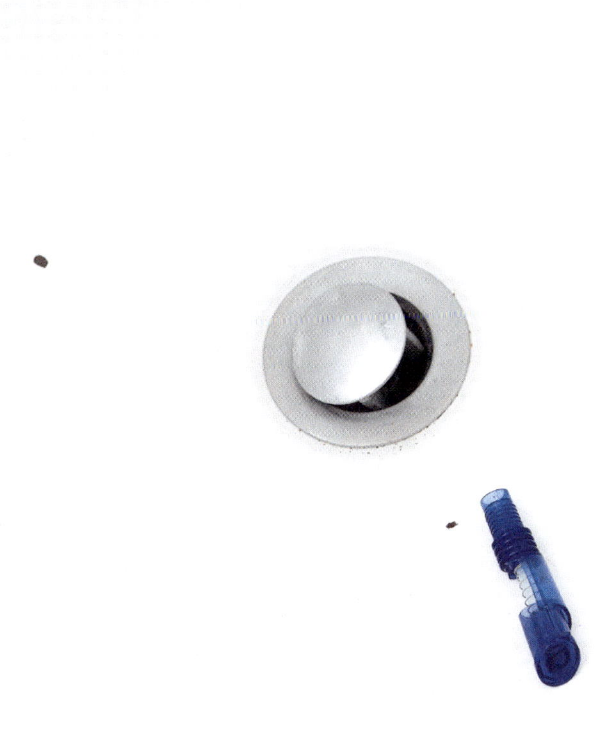

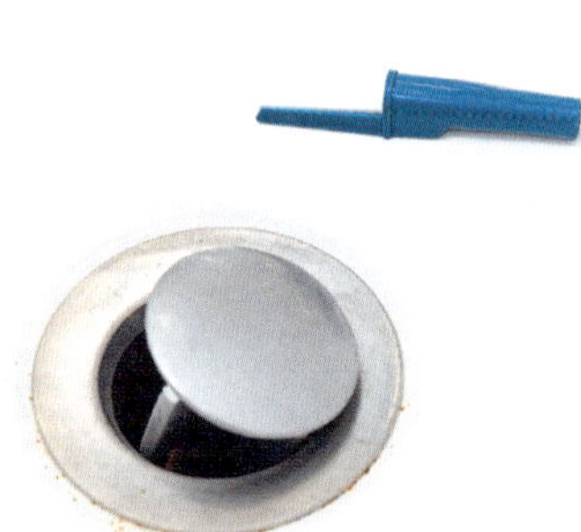

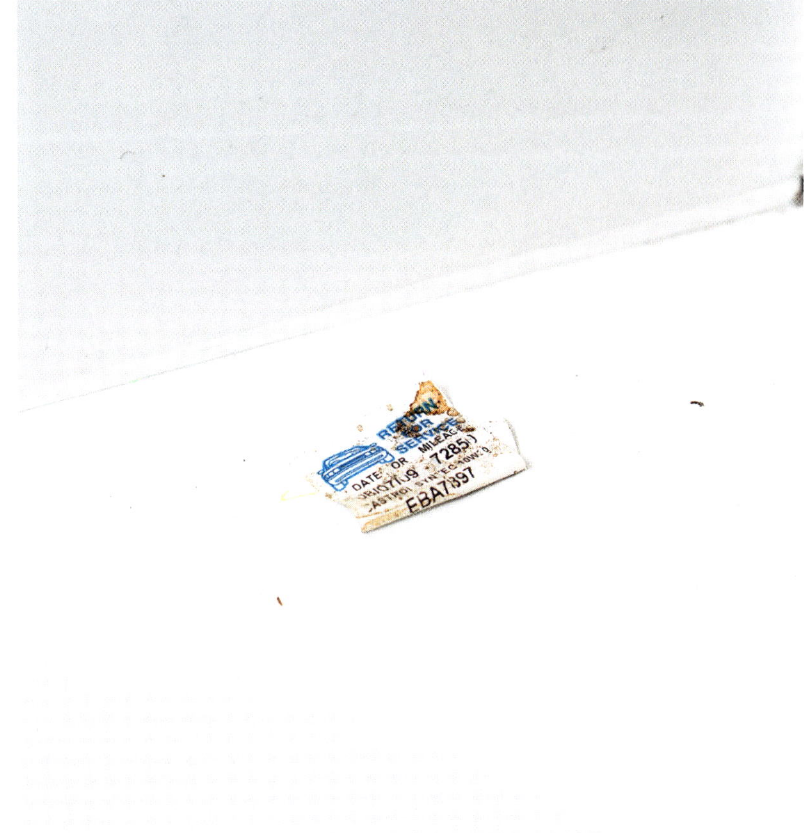
RETURN
FOR
SERVICE
DATE OR MILEAGE
7285

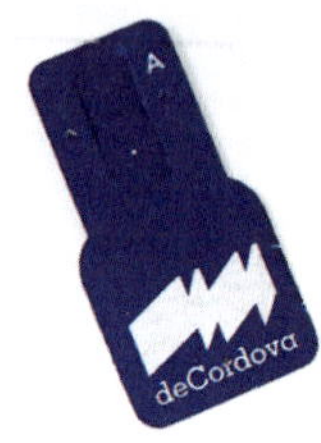
A
deCordova

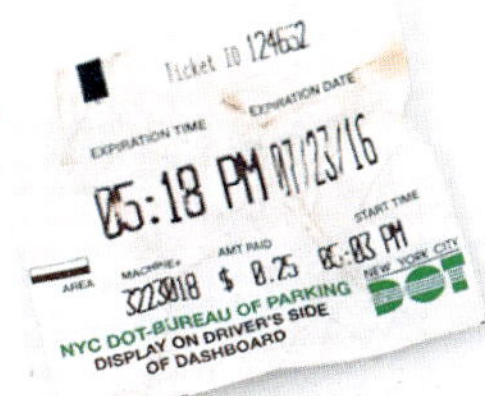
Ticket ID 124652
EXPIRATION TIME
EXPIRATION DATE
05:18 PM 07/23/16
START TIME
AREA
MACHINE#
AMT PAID
3223018 $ 0.25 05:03 PM
NEW YORK CITY
DOT
NYC DOT-BUREAU OF PARKING
DISPLAY ON DRIVER'S SIDE
OF DASHBOARD

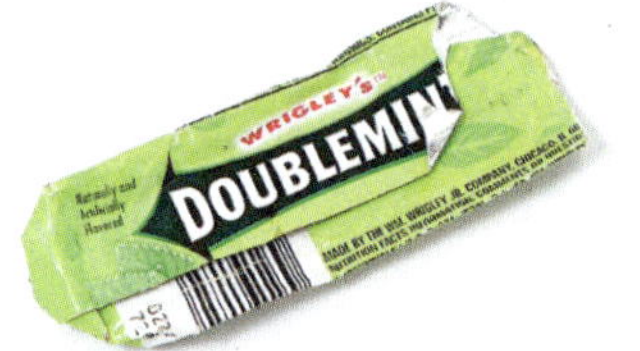
WRIGLEY'S
DOUBLEMIN

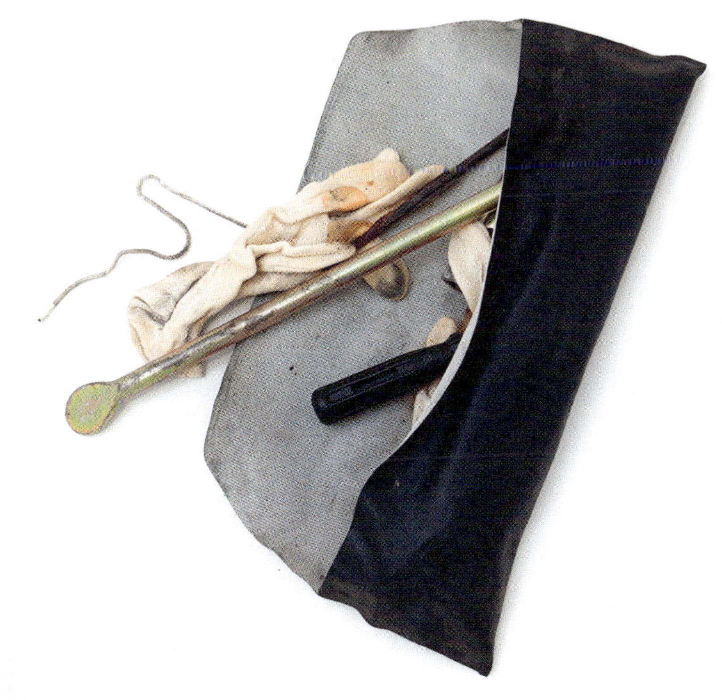

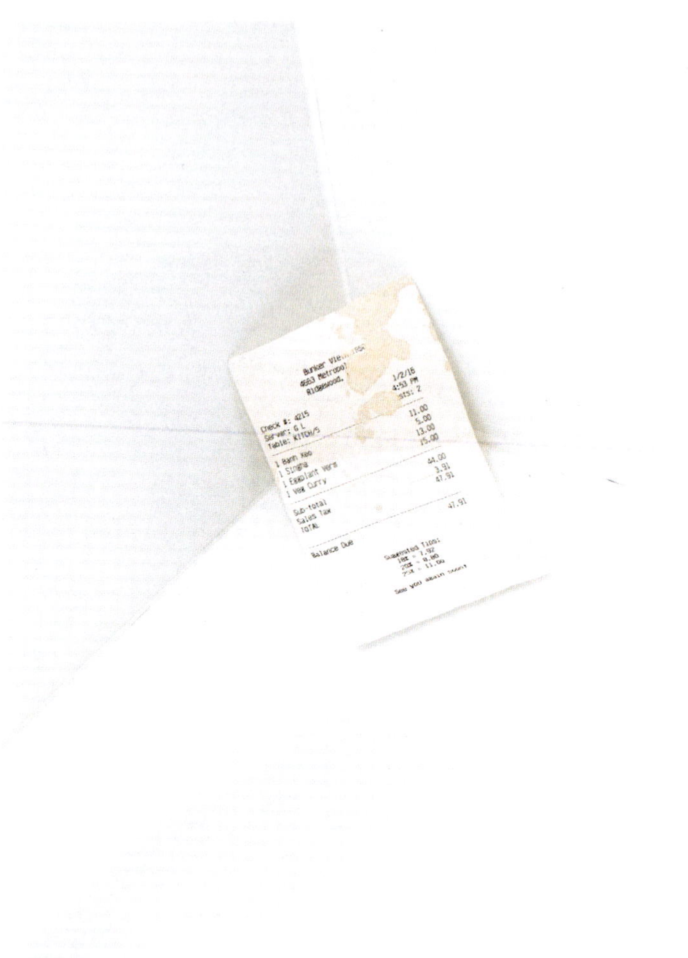
Bunker Vie
4663 Metropol
Ridgewood,
1/2/16
4:53 PM
sts: 2
Check #: 4215
Server: G L
Table: KITCH/5
11.00
5.00
13.00
15.00
1 Banh Xeo
1 Singha
1 Eggplant Vera
1 Veg Curry
44.00
3.91
47.91
Sub-total
Sales Tax
TOTAL
47.91
Balance Due
Suggested Tips:
See you again soon!

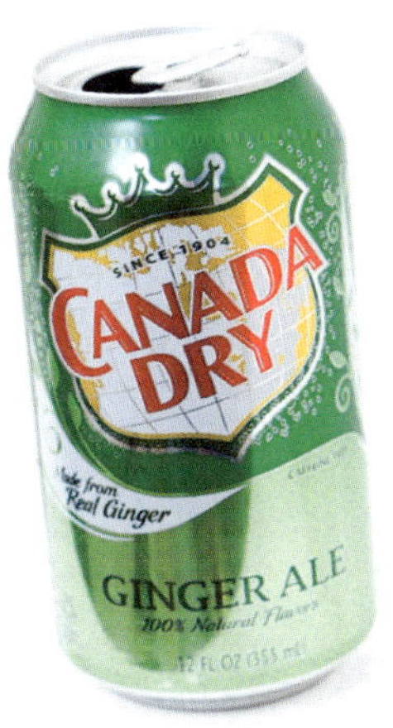
SINCE 1904
CANADA DRY
Made from Real Ginger
GINGER ALE
100% Natural Flavors
12 FL OZ (355 mL)

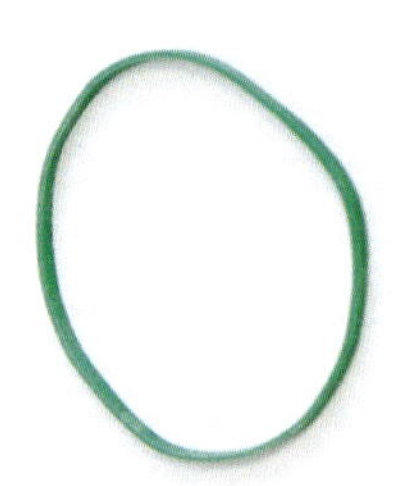

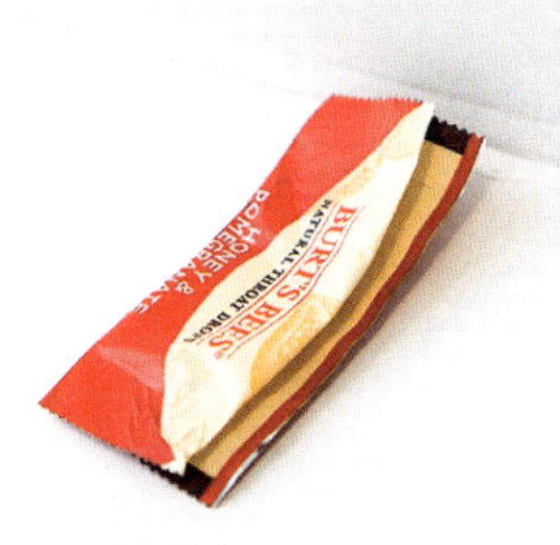
BURT'S BEES
NATURAL THROAT DROP
HONEY &
POMEGRANATE

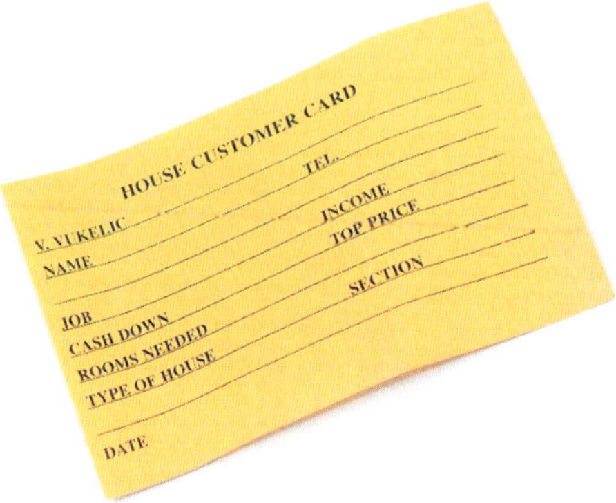

HOUSE CUSTOMER CARD

V. VUKELIC

NAME TEL.

INCOME

TOP PRICE

JOB

CASH DOWN

ROOMS NEEDED SECTION

TYPE OF HOUSE

DATE

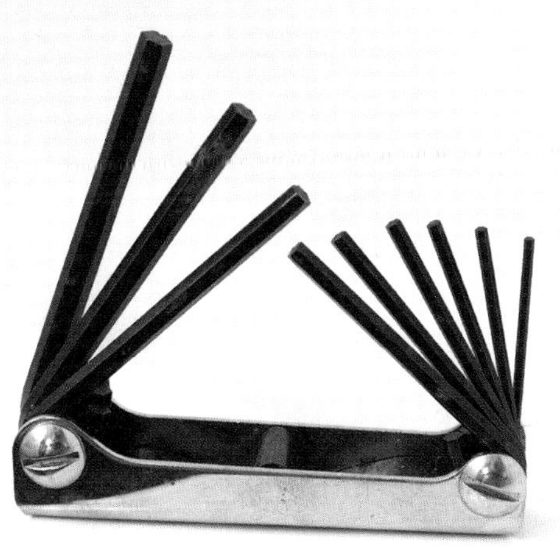

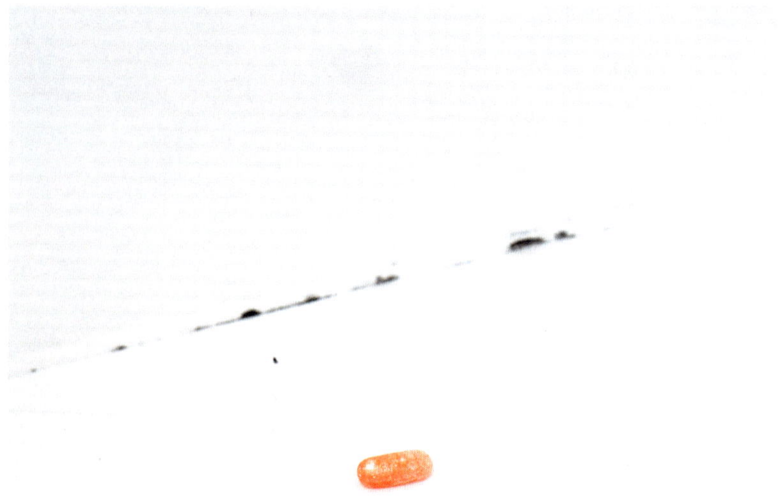

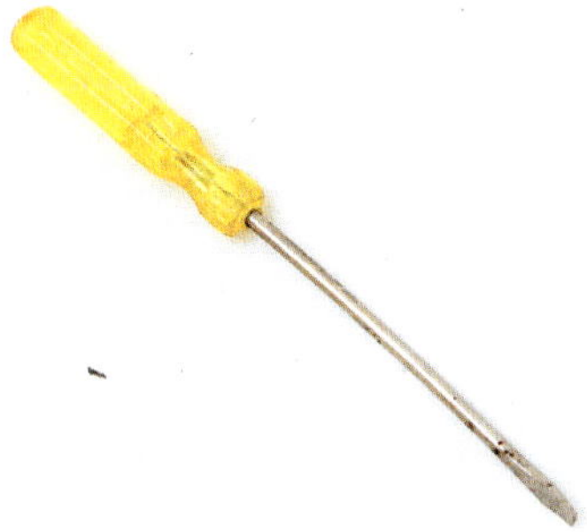

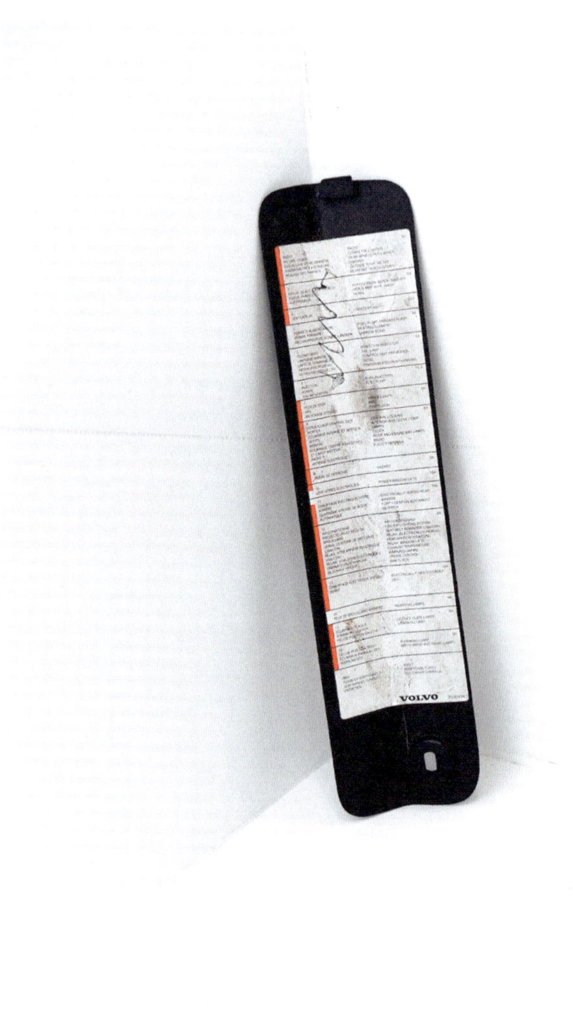
VOLVO

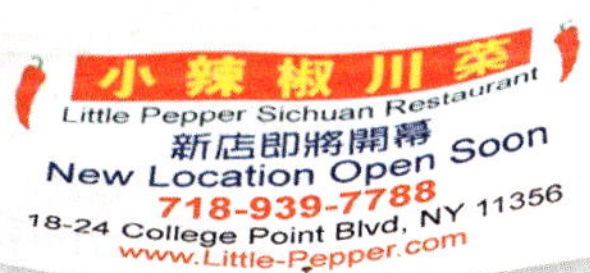

小辣椒川菜
Little Pepper Sichuan Restaurant
新店即將開幕
New Location Open Soon
718-939-7788
18-24 College Point Blvd, NY 11356
www.Little-Pepper.com

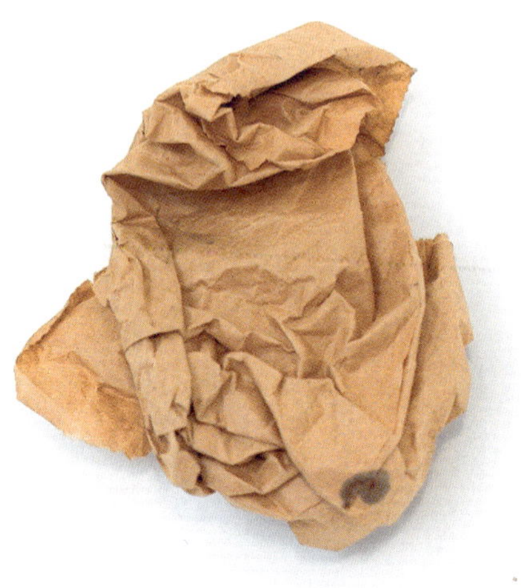

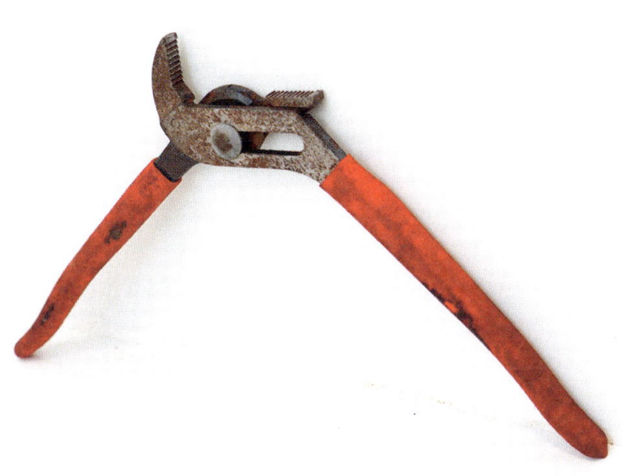

II.

The way I began thinking about narrative, it was the problem. The problem was, narrative, as such, did not exist in life, as such.

In life, things had happened. Of this I was sure. As such, things were done and were one thing. As such, they were an event. An event, as I understood it, was a whole. In an event, everything occurs as if at once, is pressed together into that term. So you can know it. A one. A whole. An event.

But narrative is something else.

In narrative, we do not know what will happen, until later. Part of what occurs is withheld, and then it is constructed, before our very eyes. In narrative, what occurs happens. I know this seems a bit redundant, but please bear with me. I could also write, what happens occurs. And sometimes what occurs is even part of the past. Sometimes we do know what will happen but do not know what *has* happened.

Of course, there are other parts of narrative: There is the question of who is speaking, what that person or entity can see and name, how much that person or entity knows, what that person or entity is willing to share with an audience. So it is not just the matter of rendering an event as a series of entailed actions; it is a matter of deciding why someone would begin to talk about this thing at all.

Speaking of talking, yesterday I was on the phone with someone and we were discussing stories. I can't tell you everything about what we said. The important part is the part about telling. The person I was speaking to has both a personal and a professional relationship to writing, and I guess that is true of me, too. The person I was speaking to encouraged me to say more about what I am writing in stories, and I explained that when I put things in an order, in a linear order—

an arrangement of clear causal progression, via x comes y—violence seems to come into it.

Why? this person wanted to know.

That's a good question, I said.

If I hadn't been afraid, in that moment, of seeming to know too much about my own writing, I might have pointed out a few things I recall from the history of literature. For example, in his *Poetics*, Aristotle explains that what is particular about tragedy is action. In one analogy he says that you can understand the significance—to the particular kind of plot a tragedy has—of action by thinking about visual art. He asks you to imagine a very colorful, bad painting and then to think of a simple portrait done in lines of chalk. The success of the lines in this simple chalk portrait—perhaps they are vivid because someone has drawn them casually and quickly—is the same success and vividness of action in tragedy. Of course, the tragedy may be elaborately considered. And this might be true of the chalk portrait, too. Maybe Aristotle is giving us an indication about what works in the representational arts: One should know what one is doing, but it should not appear that one has labored to do what one has done. Or, perhaps he is saying that there is a side to even the expressly representational, realistic work of art, the work of art in which we recognize ourselves, that resists being brought into the light of what we know. Here, in this line of chalk, is what we do not know about what we are. *And now*, Aristotle says, with a kind of glaring optimism, *you may look at it*.

There is more to this, to plot, to that line drawing which is not quite the same thing as narrative. Plot is, to my mind, the abstract side of narrative, but in saying this I realize that it requires unpacking. Let us, for the sake of experiment, say that we have two categories, two ways we will provisionally group some concepts and stuffs for the sake of temporary exploration. I'll call one "plot" and the other "narrative." And, in fact, I want to start by explaining what I think goes into the pile called "narrative." In narrative we find: The promise that someone will speak to tell us what has taken place. There is also something called experience, here. And it seems right to say that experience and speaking about it come to be interrelated through narrative, which is, in itself (and, therefore) not identical either to experience or to speaking about it. The reason that this is the case is that the time of speaking about experience is not identical to the time of living.

Narrative is a form of permission. And although plot is a way of organizing narrative, narrative exceeds it. There are narratives without plot, narratives where plot is narrative. Think of a song.

Plot is a pattern. It is the choice to discover the body before or after dinner, to discover the existence of the ancestor before or after marriage, to see her smiling or to only learn of it secondhand.

But I didn't come here to provide you with definitions of words you already use all the time. You don't need me for that, and I like to be useful.

So here, instead, is a story.

Once upon a time there were four people. They met on an afternoon in June in a small American city. They had never met one another before. That afternoon, the four people participated in an event together. After the event was over, it was late, and the four people returned to their lodging in a car owned by one of the people, let us call him M. Driving back to their lodging in the car owned by M., they were stopped by a police officer, who requested that M. have working brake lights, writing him a citation that was to be revoked upon replacement of brake-light bulbs. It was dark when they were stopped, which was more or less ominous and more or less alarming, variously, for the car's occupants. The police officer walked swiftly toward the car.

Returning to their lodgings a little later, two developments of note occurred among the four people: One person left the group in order to join a lover. One person decided to go to bed. M. and another member of the group resolved to do an art project together. They would remove all of the contents of his car, anything not bolted down or otherwise attached to the body. They would then catalogue these objects.

One person having left, and M. and another person having come to their resolution regarding the car, the remaining three persons, M. and the two others (one of whom simply wished to sleep), went, at last, to bed. The next morning, when they awoke, they discovered that the futon M. was sleeping on (it was a rented house), was full of bedbugs.

Over the course of the coming days the remaining three persons would: launder all the possessions they had brought with them over and over again, commiserate endlessly, move house. Also, M. and the person previously indicated would make a number of different catalogues of the contents of M.'s car.

Things that are barely objects and are hard to describe, from the interior of Matthew Connors's car (but the task of accounting for them makes them feel like significant objects):

1. NYC DOT parking voucher, 5:45pm, 12/29/08; $00.75
2. NYC DOT parking voucher, 4:24pm, 12/18/12; $1.00
3. Partial NYC DOT parking voucher, 4:28pm, 12/31/12; $00.50
4. Flat white circular chocolate wrapper paper
5. Plastic bottleneck covering for Starbucks coffee drink
6. Ricola green tea echinacea sugar-free cough drop wrapper
7. "NO REFUNDS DUE TO WEATHER" Route 290 Gate 06/24/2017; 5:48pm; $8.00 cash paid
8. San Pellegrino Melograno e Arancia can cover
9. Burt's Bee's natural throat drops, "Honey & Pomegranate" wrapper
10. JP Auto Service 429 Centre Street Jamaica Plain, MA 02130, $10.00
11. Whole Foods Napkin, crumpled and used
12. Tin foil crumple
13. GOLDEN TOUCH CAR WASH & LUBE, 296 4th Ave, (718) 855-3400, 08/07/09

14. Unidentifiable blue tape piece (translucent)
15. Dried banana stem (some dried fibers at bottom)
16. Ricola original herb yellow cough drop wrapper
17. Plastic tooth-shaped fragment, white with what appears to be black spray paint
18. Blue translucent plastic pen part, top with spring
19. 5:18pm, 7/23/16, parking validation $00.25, 5:03pm
20. Dried (beech?) leaf
21. Unidentifiable paper scrap (dirty and with no print), blank
22. Sony headphones minder made of black plastic
23. Crumpled white paper towel fragment
24. Unidentifiable black plastic fragment, probably from car interior
25. De Cordova plastic museum tag, blue, marked “A”
26. Tan plastic fragment, some kind of cover for something, textured front, like fake leather
27. Paper fragment that may or may not contain snot, folded in half
28. CVS pharmacy receipt for Reese’s King Size, half and half, Tropicana with calcium, 10/01/2013, 4:25pm
29. Compostable spoon handle
30. Burt’s Bee’s natural throat drops, “Honey & Pomegranate,” wrapper
31. An anti-nausea remedy (car-sickness prevention medicine), white with degraded coating, coding also worn off

32. Same as above, with water-resistant packaging
33. Empty packaging (same as above)—“Dimenhydrinate”
34. Knob cover, or a hose cap, or radio dial; light black, a paper-fine plastic, ridged
35. “Welcome to IKEA” “Returns & Exchange” ticket, number 111, 2015-12-06, 12:14pm
36. Unidentifiable plastic cover, pale gray, “HEWILA”
37. “MoMA PS1” sticker

38. Green rubber band
39. Flimsy cardboard fragment with printed lattice pattern, probably from a Kleenex box
40. Partial white paper drinking straw wrapper, lightly stained
41. Dried piece of tape
42. Red plastic zip tie very dried
43. Beige plastic fragment
44. Beige plastic fragment
45. Beige plastic fragment
46. Unidentifiable black plastic fragment, seems too heavy to be a spoon handle
47. Black and white plastic pen cap
48. Very dirty white paper circular candy wrapper
49. One bobby pin
50. Pen interior/stick (for ink)
51. Dried green rubber band
52. Candy wrapper fragment; "Gluten" "Butter" visible
53. Revolting paper fragment
54. AUTOPART INTERNATIONAL ProTUNE OIL FILTER, Next Service Due: 116723 Mileage: 8/22/17
55. Blue plastic translucent pen top
56. Drinking straw cover fragment "TH PICK"
57. Dirty toothpick
58. Candy wrapper fragment "ees, Inc 27709"
59. Black plastic pen top
60. Beige plastic fragment, small and triangular
61. "Coffee" translucent and brown plastic fragment
62. Soda can tab
63. Revolting lint-covered almond
64. Four fuses, two red and two white
65. "MoMA PS1" sticker
66. Old wrapped Ricola "Echinacée thé vert" cough drop
67. Clear pushpin
68. Small screw
69. Two band aid wrappers

70. Really disgusting straw wrapper, very dirty
71. Six or seven dried leaves
72. White plastic pen part
73. Brown paper fragment
74. Tiny plastic fragment beige
75. Tiny gross paper towel fragment
76. Translucent toothpick wrapper
77. Tape with feathers stuck to it
78. TUMS wrapper fragment "sodium fr"
79. White paper fragment, somewhat heavy duty but not very
80. Tiny dried orange peel fragment, so dried it does not smell anymore
81. Something that appears to be a dried piece of fruit skin but is difficult to identify, seems slightly damp, dark red, nearly black
82. Piece of tape, very dried and matte
83. White plastic fragments that appear to be tines of a fork that have been broken off, but it's a pretty large fork, or was
84. What appears to be a currant but is probably a very dry grape
85. Small bark fragment
86. Very degraded chewing gum wrapper
87. Unidentifiable piece of degraded paper, soft and somewhat dirty, with a single piece of dog hair on it
88. Drinking straw wrapper fragment with flake of dried leaf on it and one piece of dog hair and a piece of fluff stuck to it
89. Dried leaf fragment, dark greenish grayish brown
90. Very dirty and degraded piece of either paper or tape, difficult to determine what it is
91. Tiny fragment of foil
92. White lint ball, soft, slightly fluffy, more pleasing than other pieces of rubbish
93. Tear of paper towel

94. Eight assorted wood fibers, different colors, brown and yellow
95. Small screw and nut and washer
96. What appears to be a paint fragment with a wood fragment and possibly a tiny piece of candy (hot pink) attached to it
97. Paper towel wisp

I know that I can do a better job with the story.

So, yes, it was June of 2017, several summers ago. I am a writer, and at the time I was careening from residency to residency, desperate not to be in New York City, less because of the heat, which was unbearable, than because of the problem of New York always feeling exactly the same (I was born and grew up there), which was in its own way different but unbearable, too.

I was in Ithaca, where I was to teach.

In New York, things were phones. What I mean is, things were: a sea of information combed through by some formulas. What rose to the top was determined by [one's previous searches, previous click-based appreciations, plus algorithmic special sauce—and don't forget that unfathomable data trove, at once far off and extraordinarily immediate]. Everything got to a person; you did not have to go and look for anything. Everything was a repetition one had not chosen; automated fate. Nothing happened, in the constancy of the event, its stale novelty. There was no surprise.

I had the strange sensation, when I met Matt—Matthew Connors—owner of the car, of having met him before. In fact, I *could* have met him before, we had friends in common, it was quite possible, it's true; but I had not.

This isn't really so important.

Anyway, Matt and I have since spoken about the exercise, our exercise. One of the things that he's said to me is that it was a way to get out of the problem of having to "make art"—but given the fact this was his car, a thing he owns, he was irrevocably attached to it, present somehow. But I'm not sure this exhausts his reasons. And it was not really up to me, given to me, to know them. I was just there to scrutinize the dust and endless Ricola wrappers.

To allow someone, or a group of people, to remove everything not bolted down from one's car and to sift through it is an anomalous and generous gesture. Analogies exist with permitting acquaintances to read one's diary or search one's home. A car is, even, like a house; it's a shelter, a dresser drawer.

Is what Matt did a way of saying, "I trust you to imagine that you could have lived this, too?" Or, is it a way of saying, "Even I am not entirely sure what it will have meant to have owned/touched/manipulated/forgotten these things"?

If I were an art historian, which I am not, I could go into all sorts of paroxysms about conceptualism and the location/identity of art work—art-working—but I feel that's a rather dry route and I prefer to identify as someone who's writing about writing, rather than as someone who's writing about art.

There is something about a sentence I wrote just a moment ago, in the previous section—something in the verb tense that relates to what I am confusedly attempting to explain about the project of not just telling but specifically writing stories now—for indeed it makes a difference. "It will have meant. . . ." The verb tenses cross one another: In the future, the past takes form. It might also be a way of describing what I think Matt is doing with his semi-archaeological photographs—that are evidentiary without being cold. One could discuss pareidolia, talk about the objects as faces, but you could also see these images as documents from a moment at which the past is asked to coalesce, to become, if for a speculative future viewer, less inchoate, to obtain a positioned form like a skein or delicate shell, a translucent carapace.

Maybe only Matt can see this. Although we can see things in the images he has made—see that they are beautifully composed—part of what we are seeing is a blind spot produced by Matt's particular relationship to these objects. And some of them, truth be told, barely obtain to the status of object. We can't know what Matt knows about these things; there's a privacy here (therefore) but what I think we can see is a sort of temporal structure, one in which the past is summoned.

Nothing more obvious, perhaps. Yet there's something about the utility/abstractness of these objects, their "once utility," that thematizes this temporal structure, even as it points to something else. This utility is an analogy for a certain kind of becoming Matt enacts with his photographs—now framed by the white of the dorm-room tub, a smooth indentation *Cimex lectularius* would have trouble crawling out of, all surface and form.

Anxiety: It's a state that is both formal and not. Once it's in things, it's hard to get it out of them.

What sort of time did we acquire from the bedbugs, from the cop?

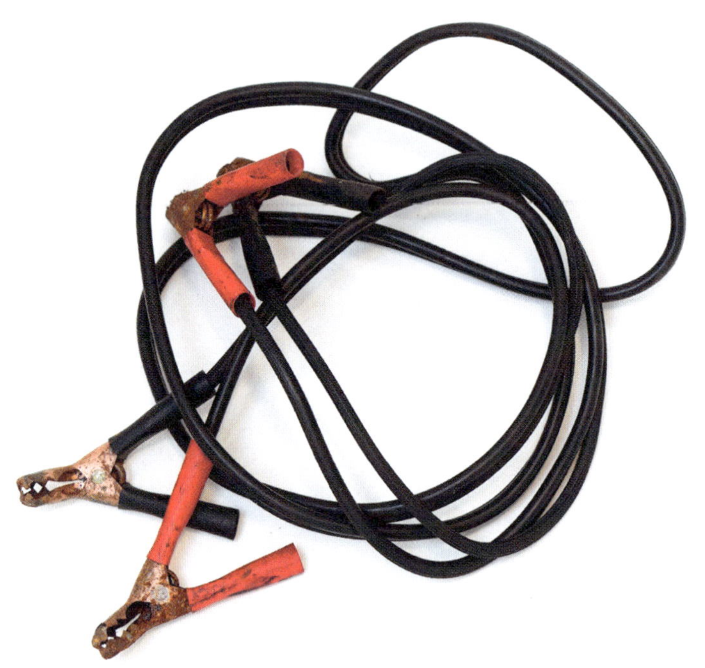

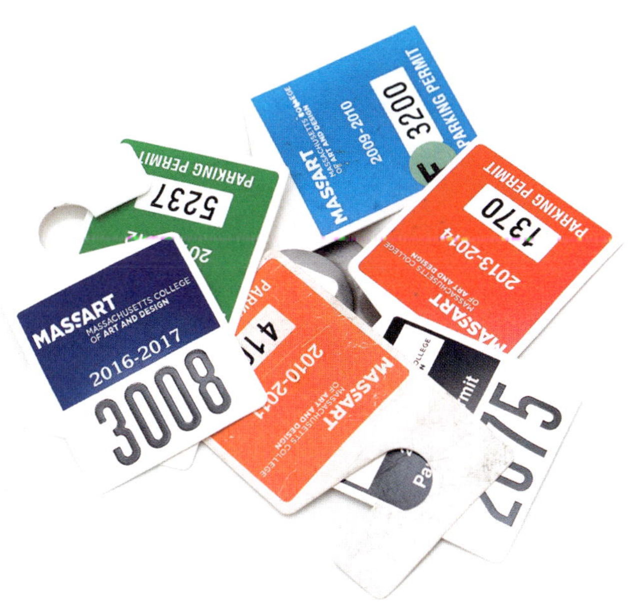
MASSART
MASSACHUSETTS COLLEGE
OF ART AND DESIGN
2016-2017
3008
PARKING PERMIT
5237
MASSART
MASSACHUSETTS COLLEGE
OF ART AND DESIGN
2009-2010
3200
PARKING PERMIT
PARKING PERMIT
1370
2013-2014
MASSART
MASSACHUSETTS COLLEGE
OF ART AND DESIGN
2010-2011
MASSART
MASSACHUSETTS COLLEGE
OF ART AND DESIGN

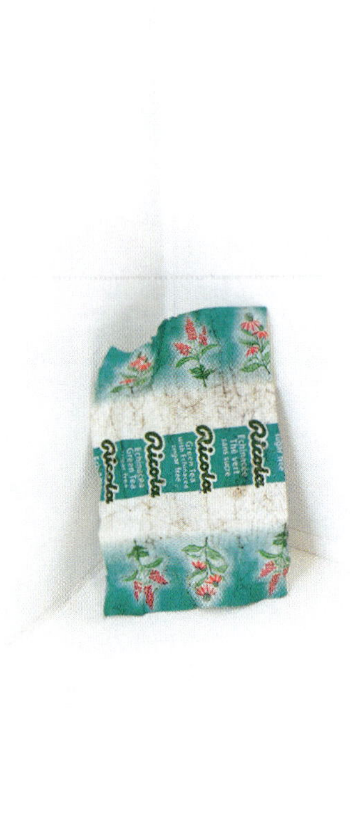
Ricola
Thé vert
sans sucre
Ricola
Green Tea
sugar free
Ricola
Echinacea
Green Tea
Ricola

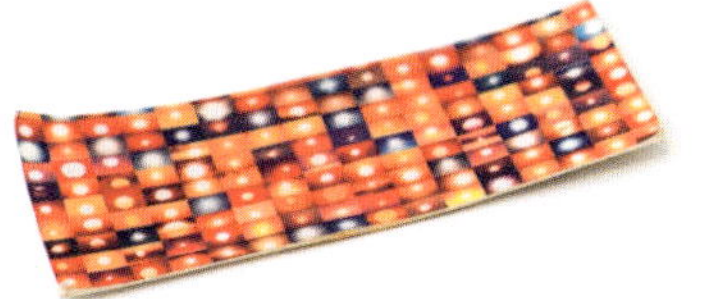

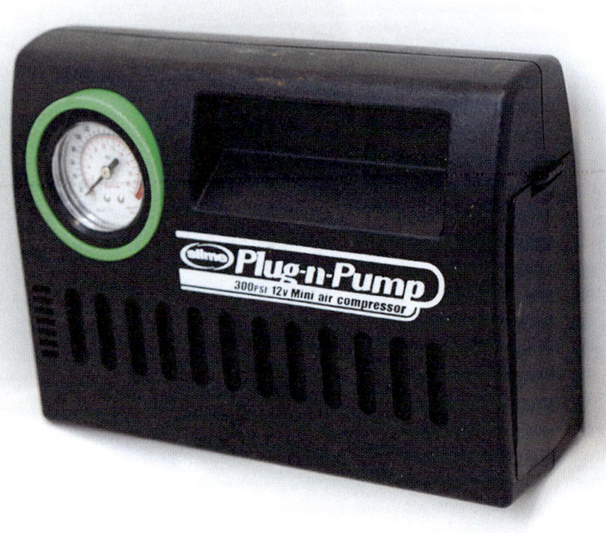
slime
Plug-n-Pump
300PSI 12v Mini air compressor

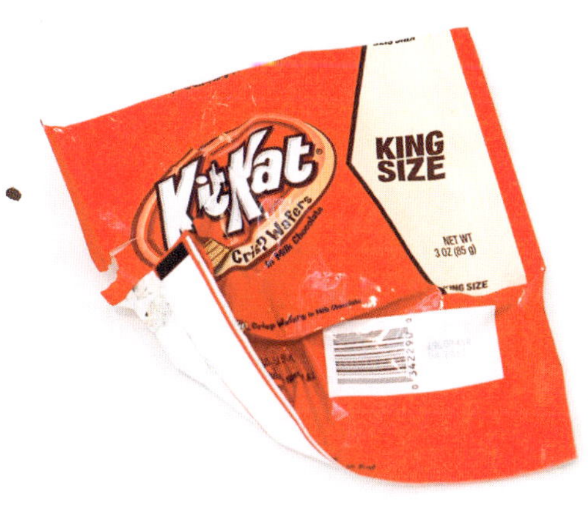
Kit Kat
Crisp Wafers
in Milk Chocolate
KING SIZE
NET WT
3 OZ (85 g)

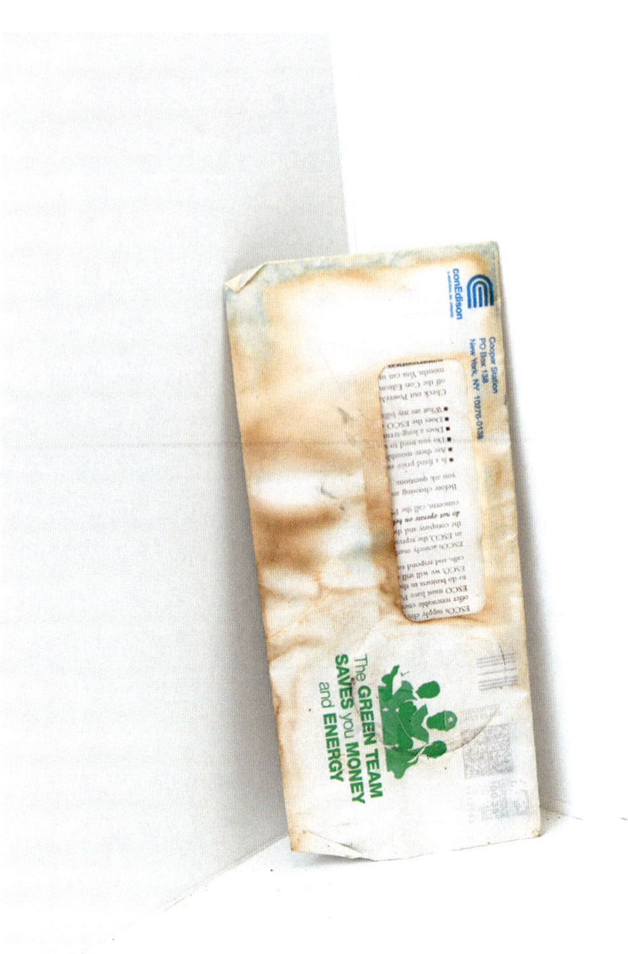
conEdison
Cooper Station
PO Box 138
New York, NY 10276-0138
The GREEN TEAM
SAVES you MONEY
and ENERGY

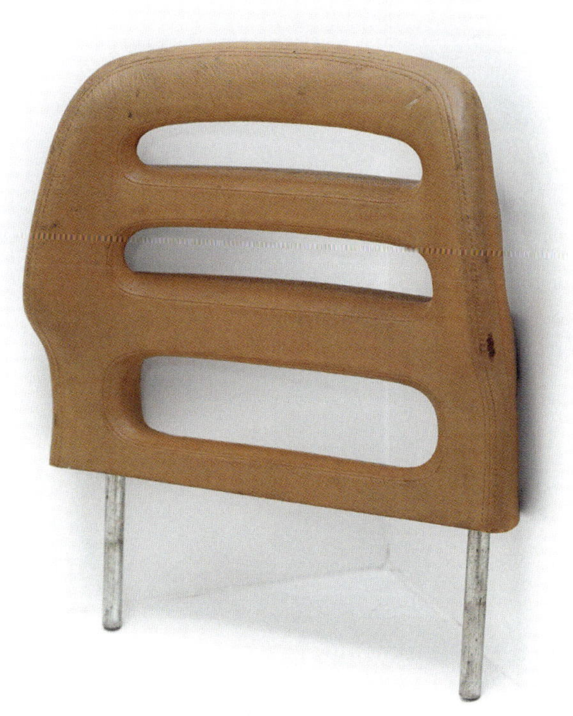

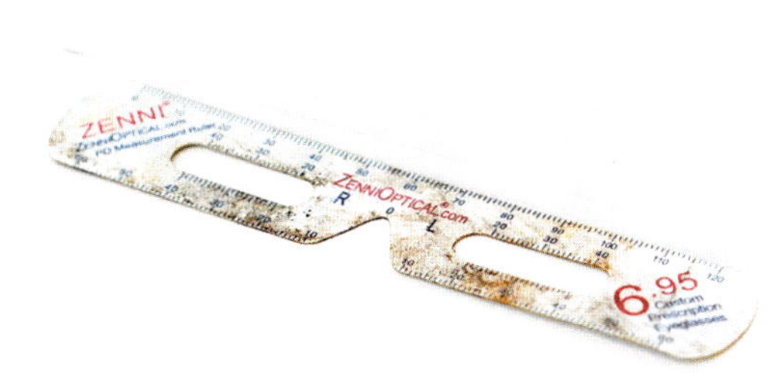
ZENNI®
ZENNIOPTICAL®com
R
0
L
6.95
Custom
Prescription
Eyeglasses

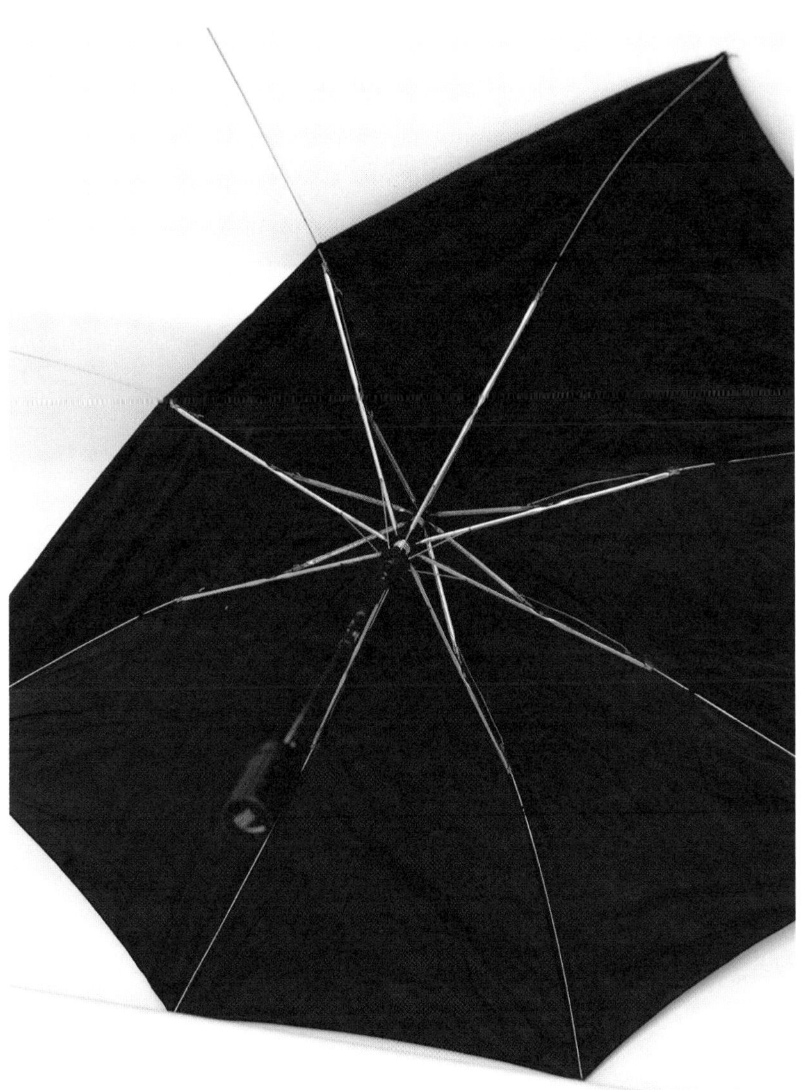

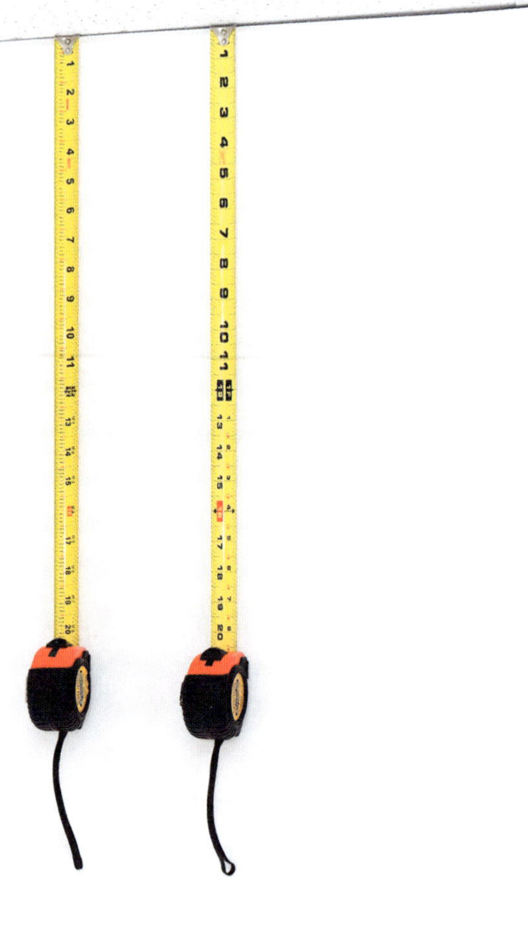

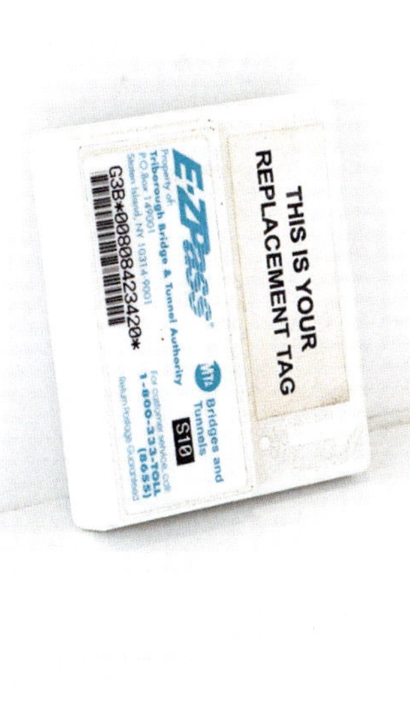
THIS IS YOUR
REPLACEMENT TAG
E-ZPass
Property of:
Triborough Bridge & Tunnel Authority
P.O. Box 149001
Staten Island, NY 10314-9001
G3B*00808423420*
MTA Bridges and Tunnels
S10
1-800-333-TOLL
(8655)

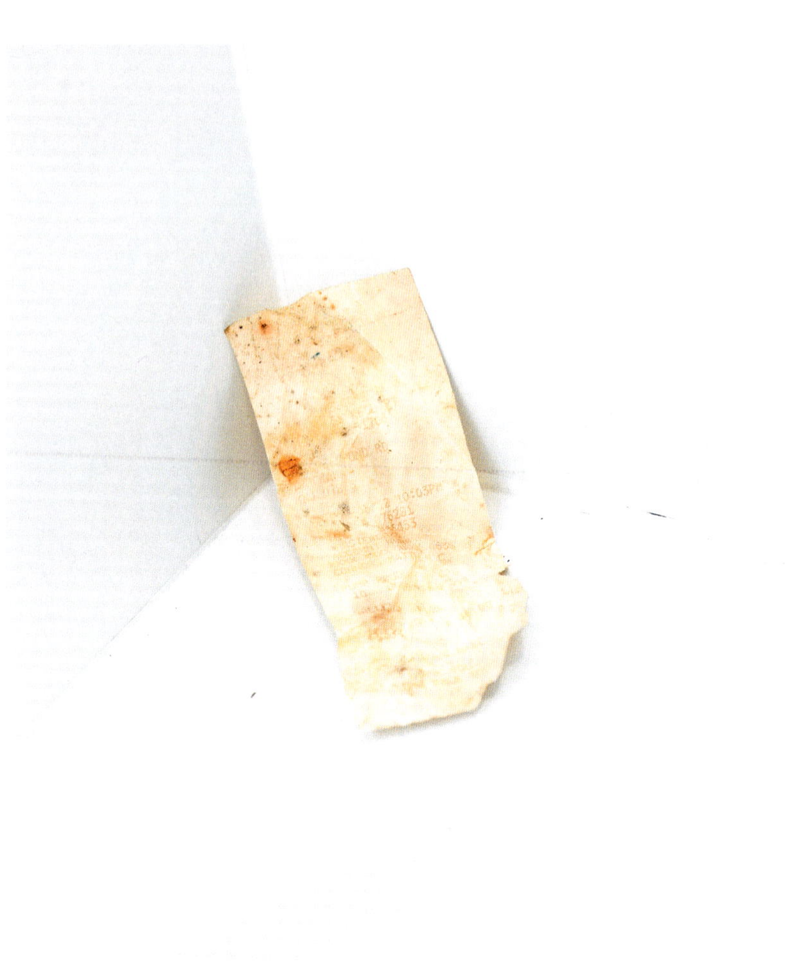

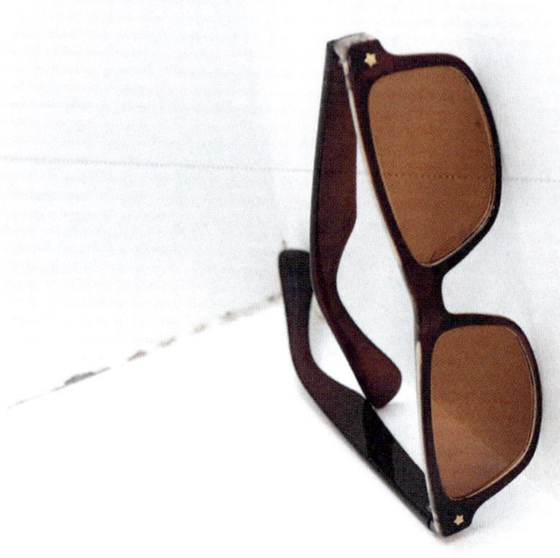

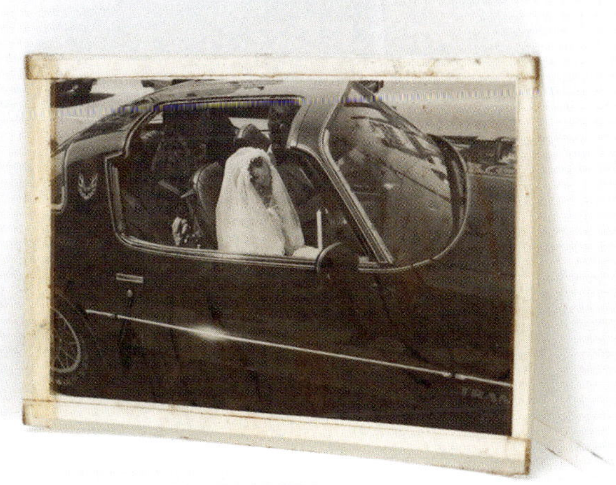

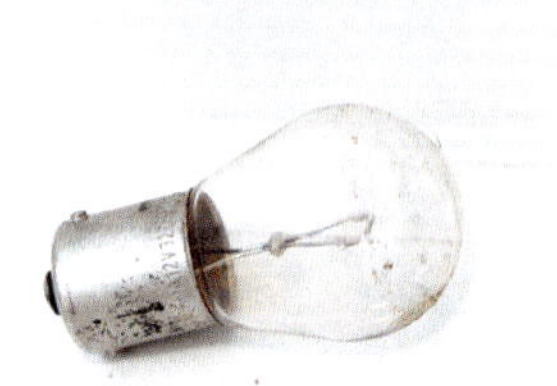

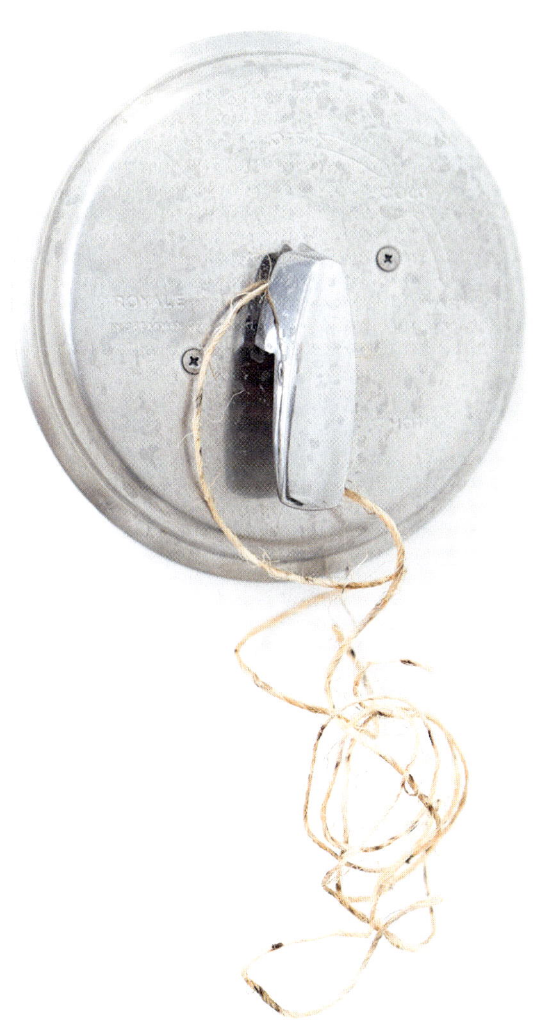

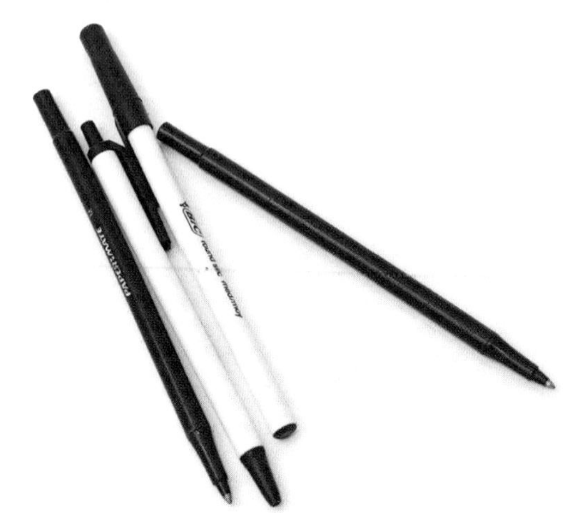

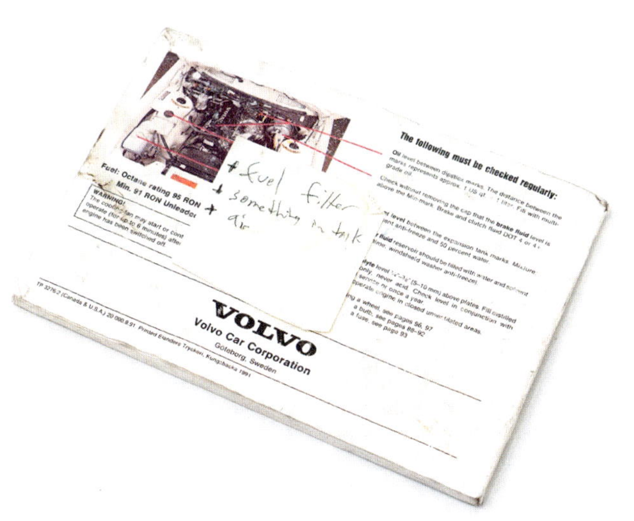
The following must be checked regularly:
Fuel: Octane rating 95 RON
Min. 91 RON Unleaded
WARNING!
+ fuel filter
+ something in tank
VOLVO
Volvo Car Corporation
Göteborg, Sweden

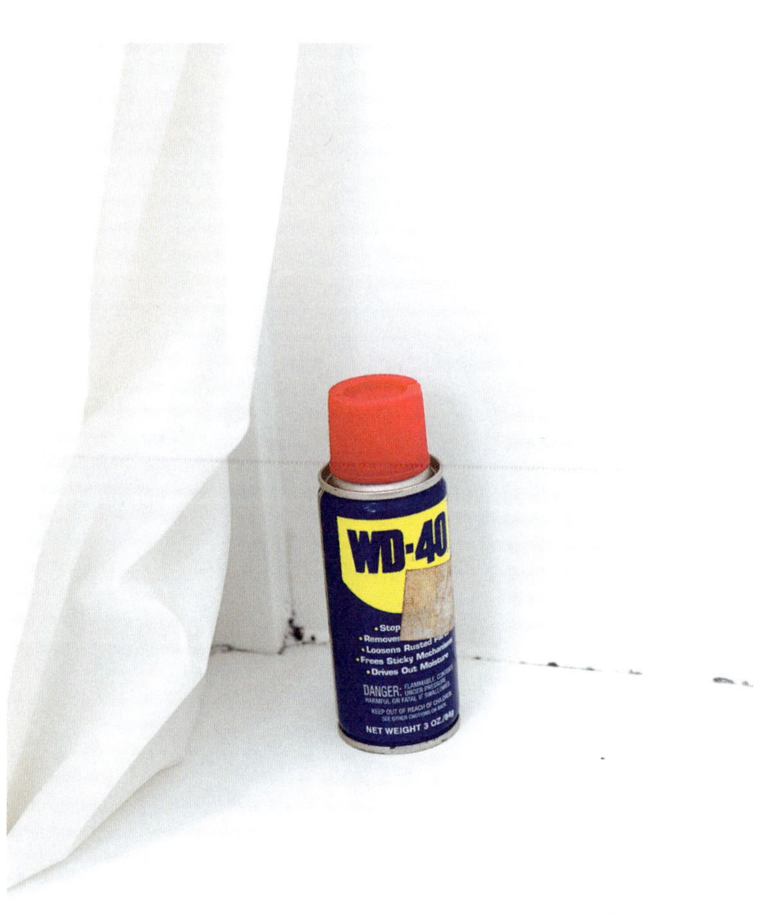
WD-40
• Loosens Rusted
• Drives Out Moisture
DANGER:
NET WEIGHT 3 OZ.

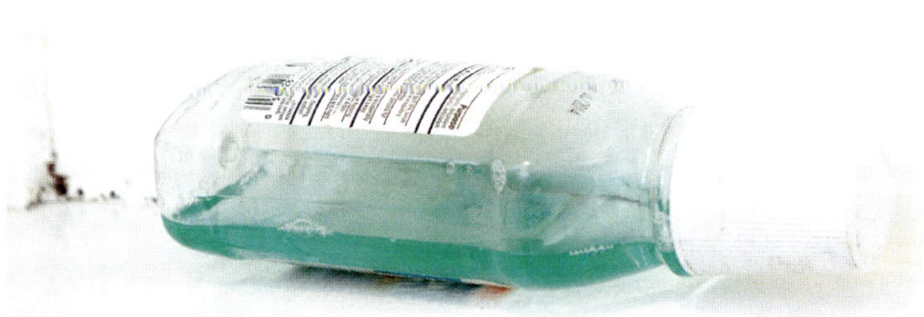

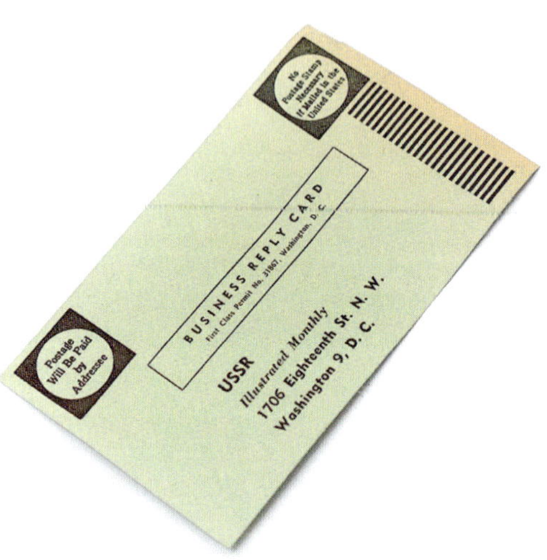

No Postage Stamp Necessary If Mailed in the United States
BUSINESS REPLY CARD
First Class Permit No. 31867, Washington, D.C.
Postage Will Be Paid by Addressee
USSR
Illustrated Monthly
1706 Eighteenth St. N. W.
Washington 9, D. C.

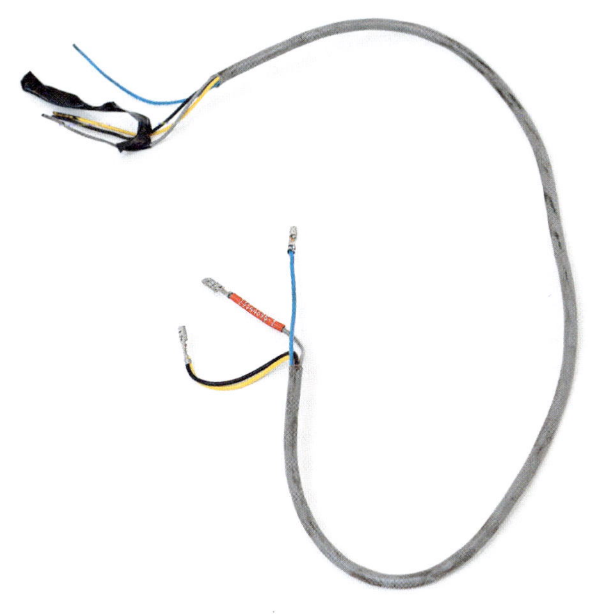

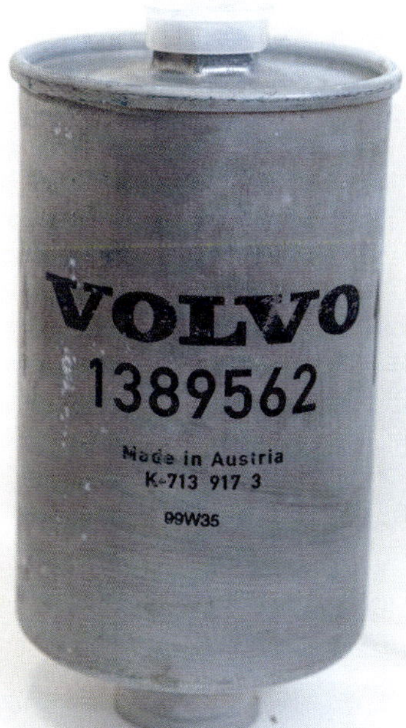
VOLVO
1389562
Made in Austria
K-713 917 3
99W35

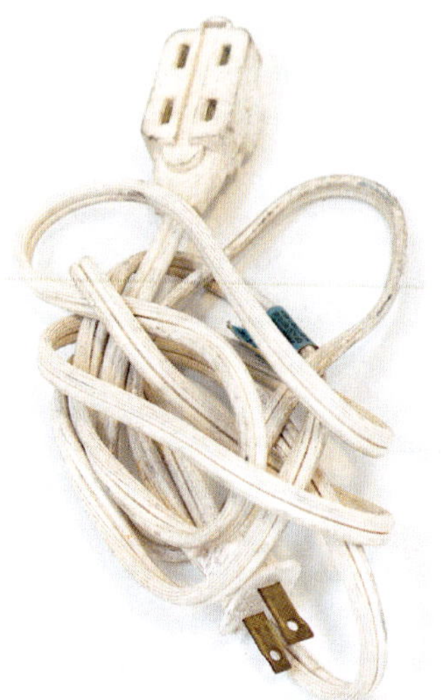

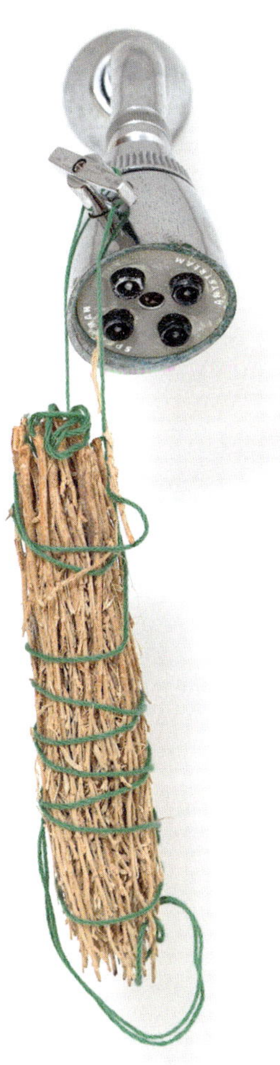

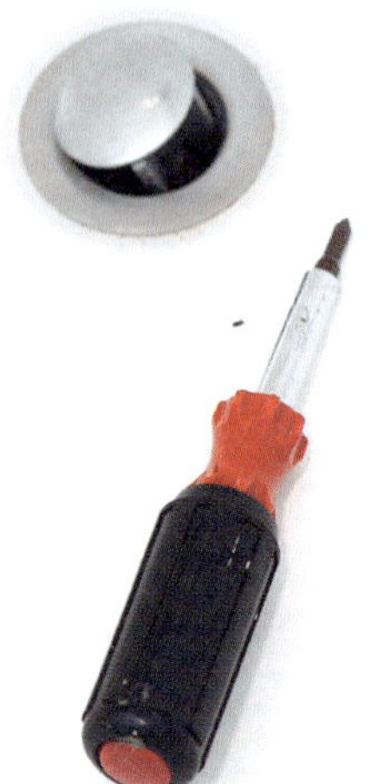

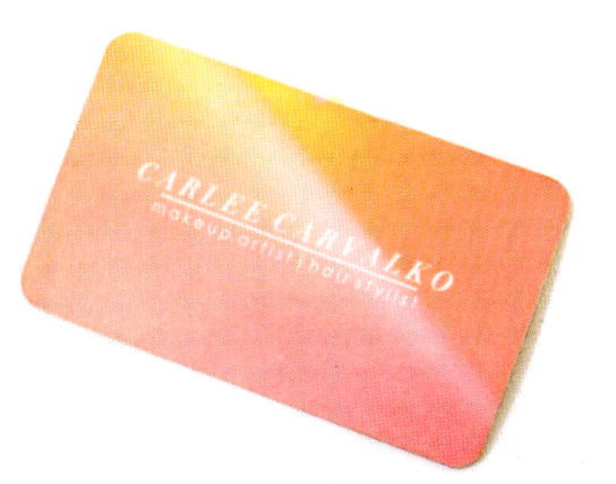
CARLEE CARVALKO
makeup artist | hair stylist

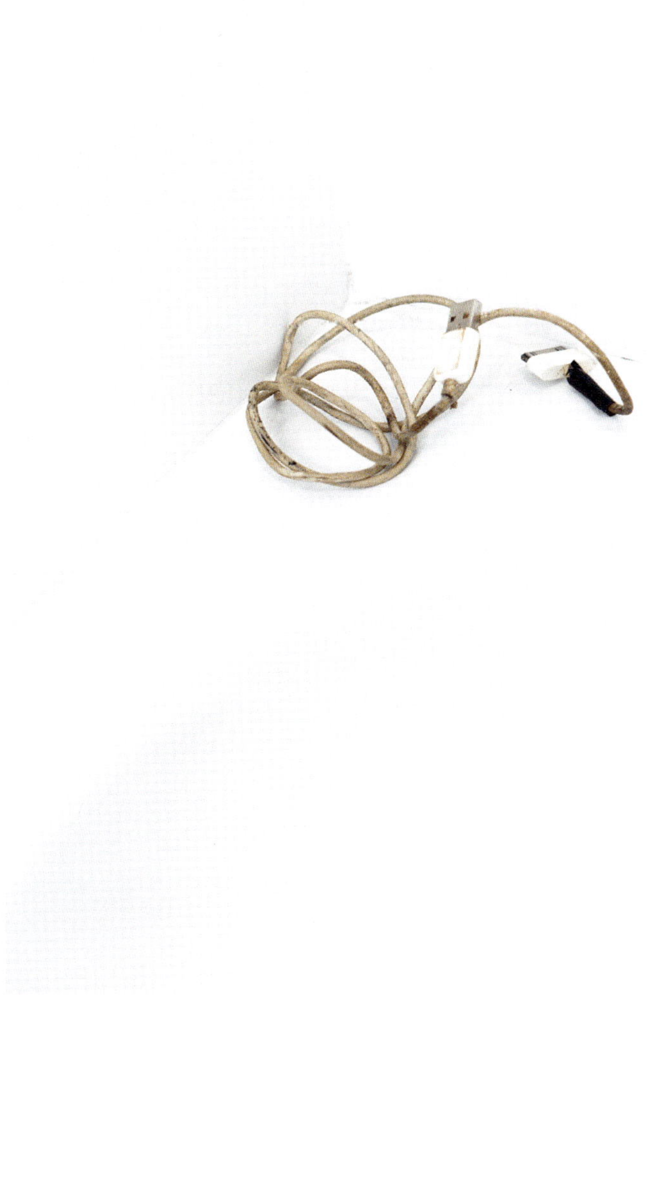

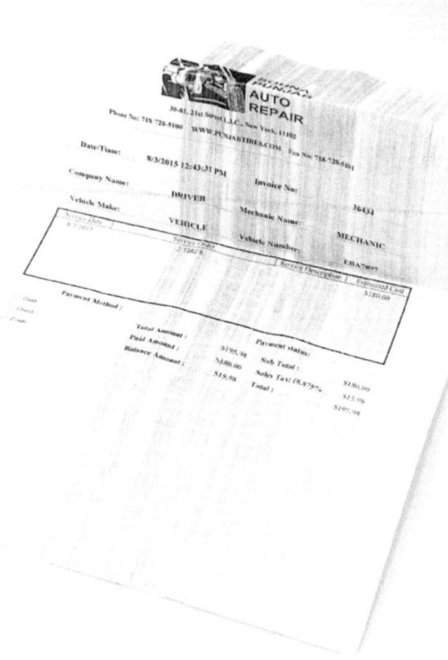
AUTO REPAIR

30-81, 21st Street L.I.C., New York, 11102

Phone No: 718-728-5100 WWW.PUNJABTIRES.COM Fax No: 718-728-5101

Date/Time: 8/3/2015 12:43:31 PM

Company Name: DRIVER

Invoice No: 36434

Vehicle Make: VEHICLE

Mechanic Name: MECHANIC

Vehicle Number: EBA7897

Service Date	Service Order	Service Description	Estimated Cost
8/3/2015	2 TIRES		$180.00

Payment Method :

Cash

Check

Credit

Total Amount : $195.98

Paid Amount : $180.00

Balance Amount : $15.98

Payment status:

Sub Total : $180.00

Sales Tax: (8.875% $15.98

Total : $195.98

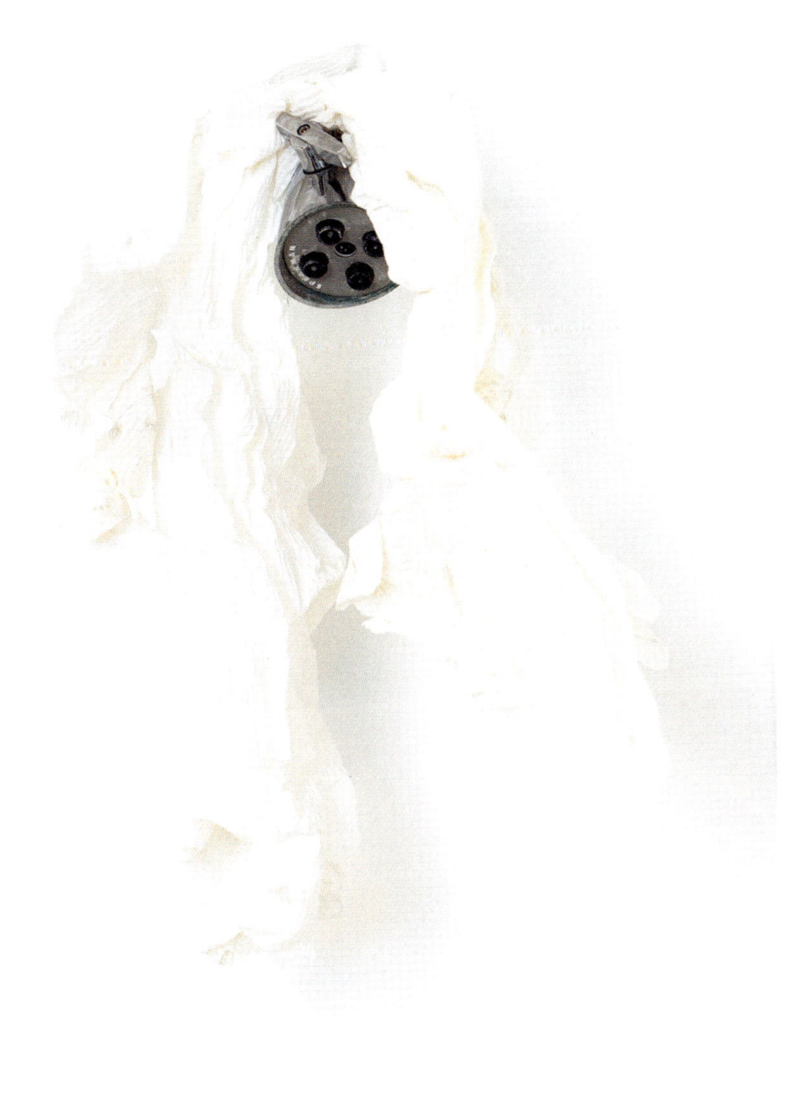

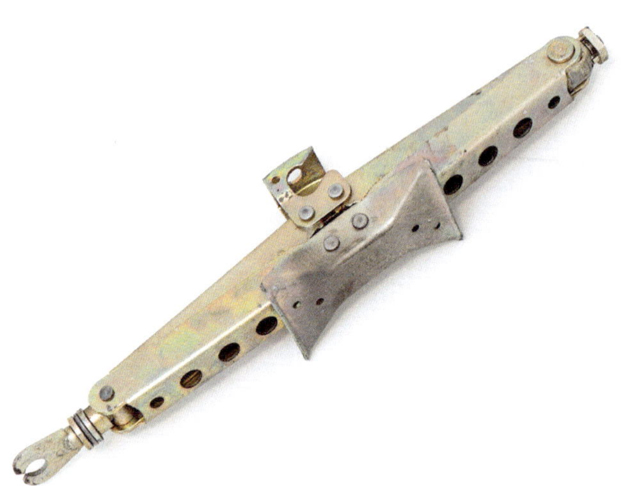

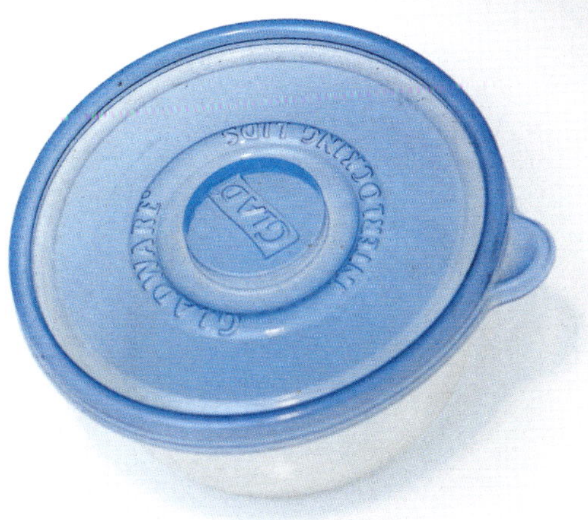
GLADWARE®
GLAD

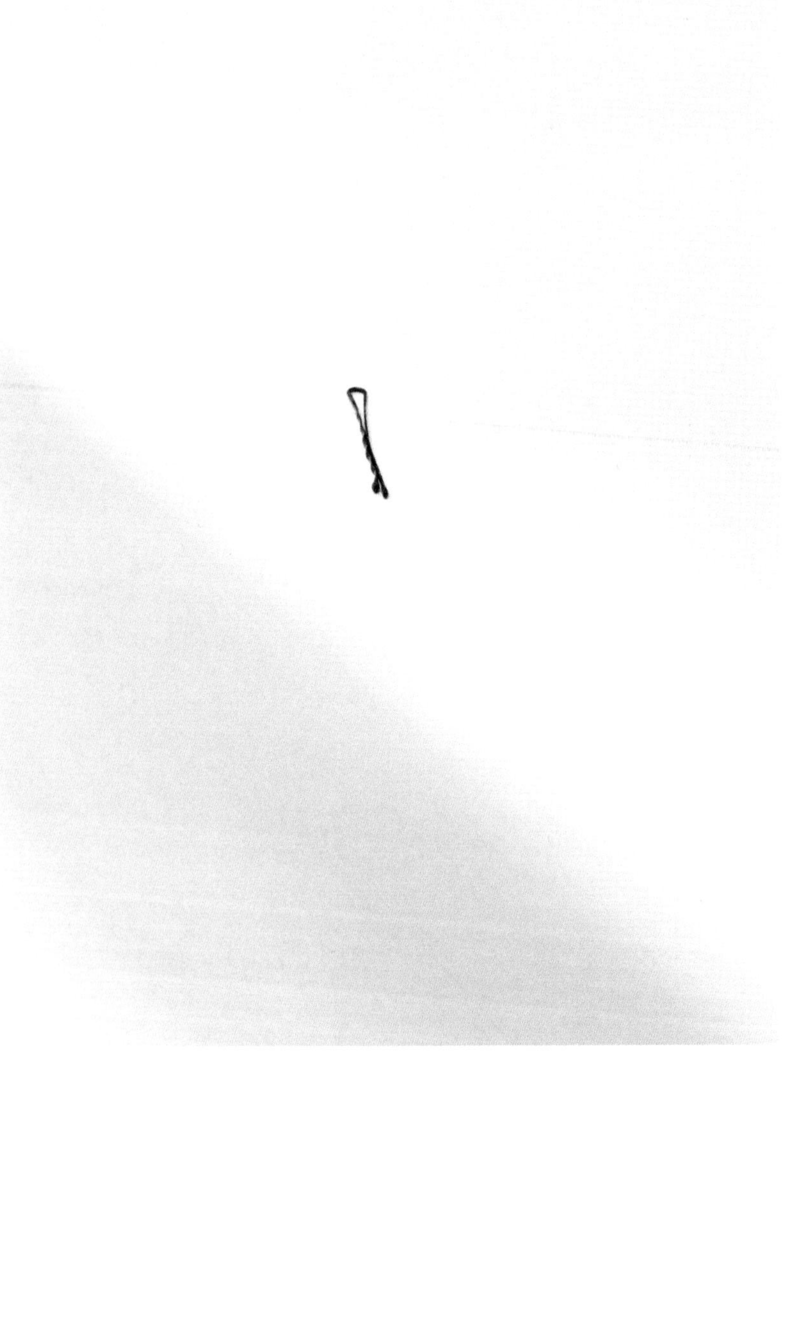

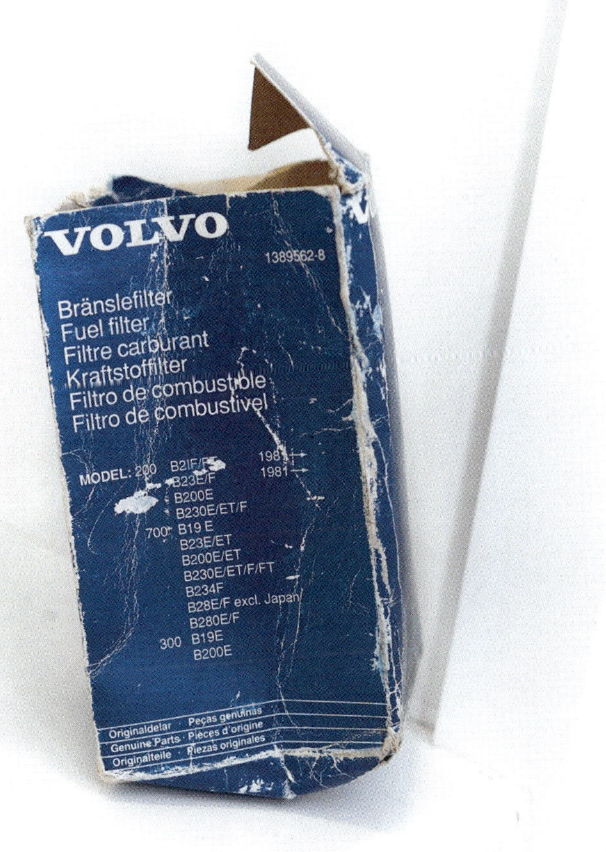
VOLVO
1389562-8
Bränslefilter
Fuel filter
Filtre carburant
Kraftstoffilter
Filtro de combustible
Filtro de combustivel
MODEL: 200
B23E/F 1981→
B200E
B230E/ET/F
700 B19 E
B23E/ET
B200E/ET
B230E/ET/F/FT
B234F
B28E/F excl. Japan
B280E/F
300 B19E
B200E
Originaldelar · Peças genuinas
Genuine Parts · Pièces d'origine
Originalteile · Piezas originales

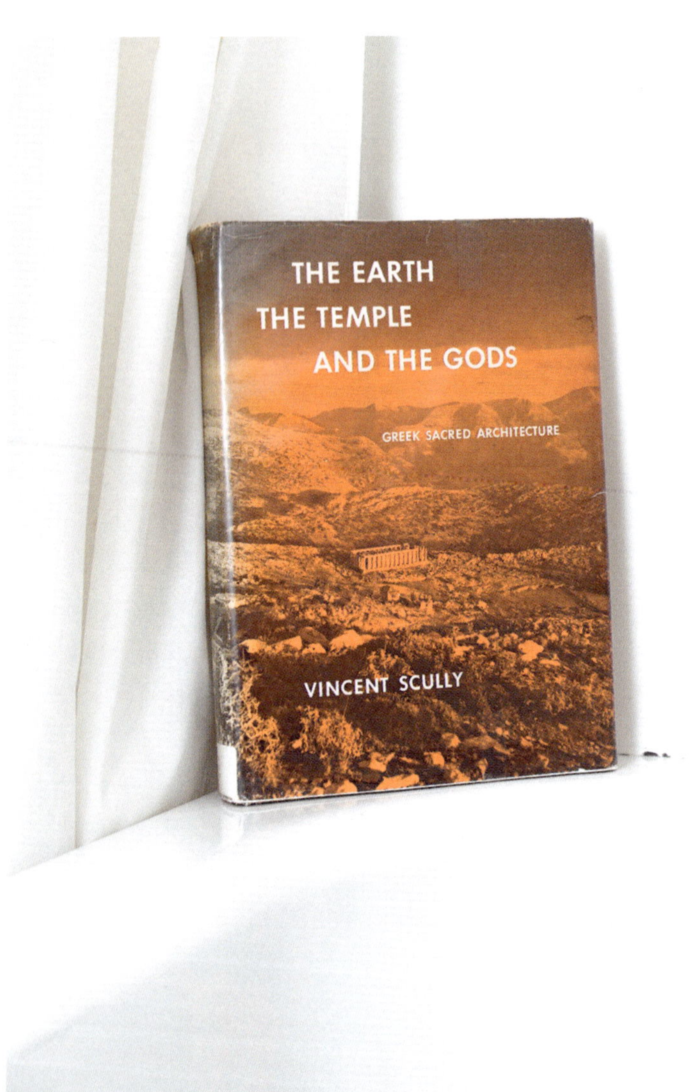
THE EARTH
THE TEMPLE
AND THE GODS
GREEK SACRED ARCHITECTURE
VINCENT SCULLY

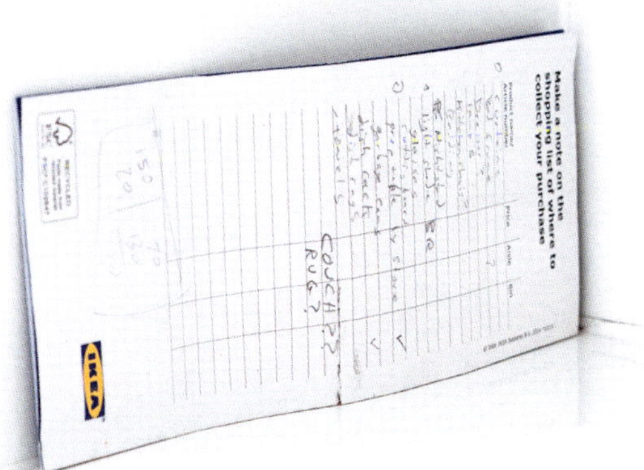
Make a note on the shopping list of where to collect your purchase
COUCH??
RUG?
IKEA

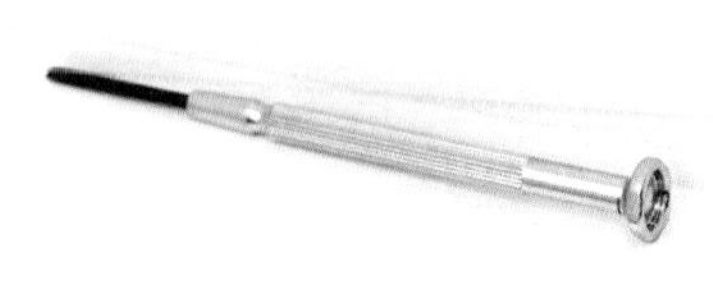

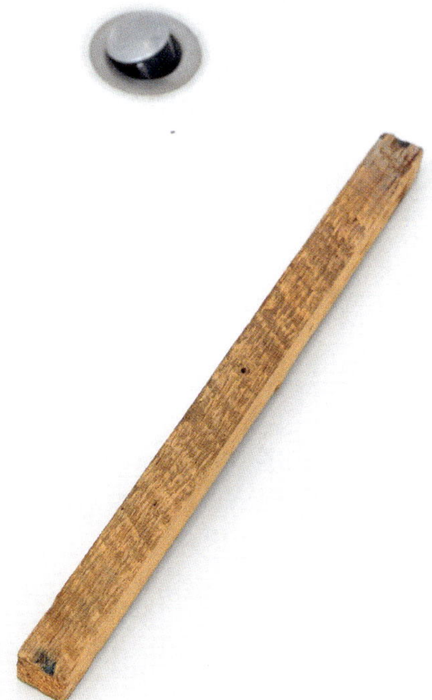

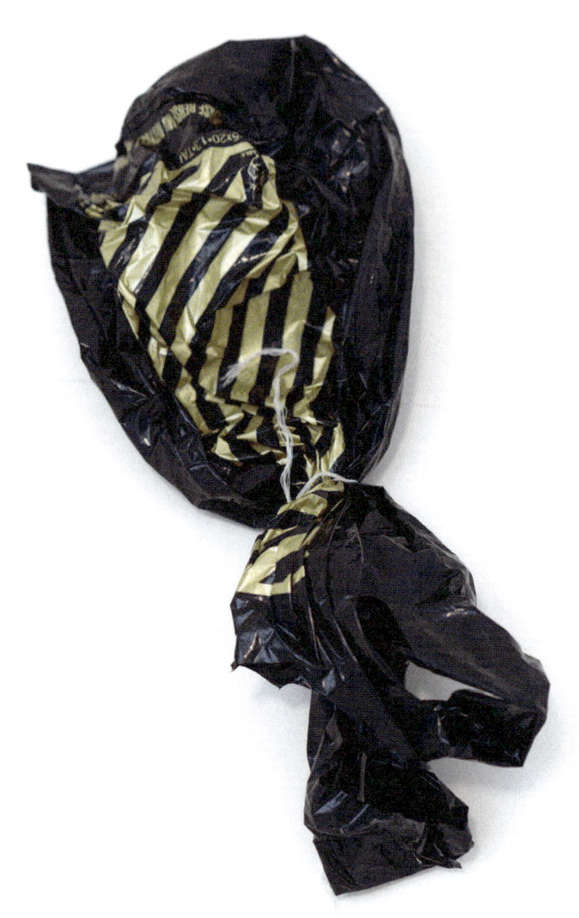

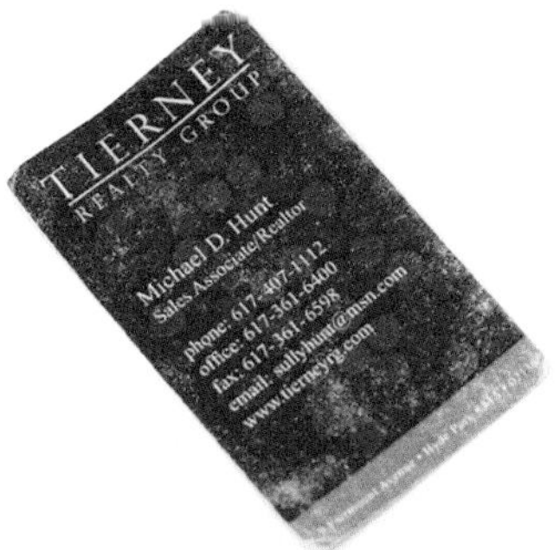
TIERNEY
REALTY GROUP
Michael D. Hunt
Sales Associate/Realtor
phone: 617-407-1112
office: 617-361-6400
fax: 617-361-6598
email: sullyhunt@msn.com
www.tierneyrg.com

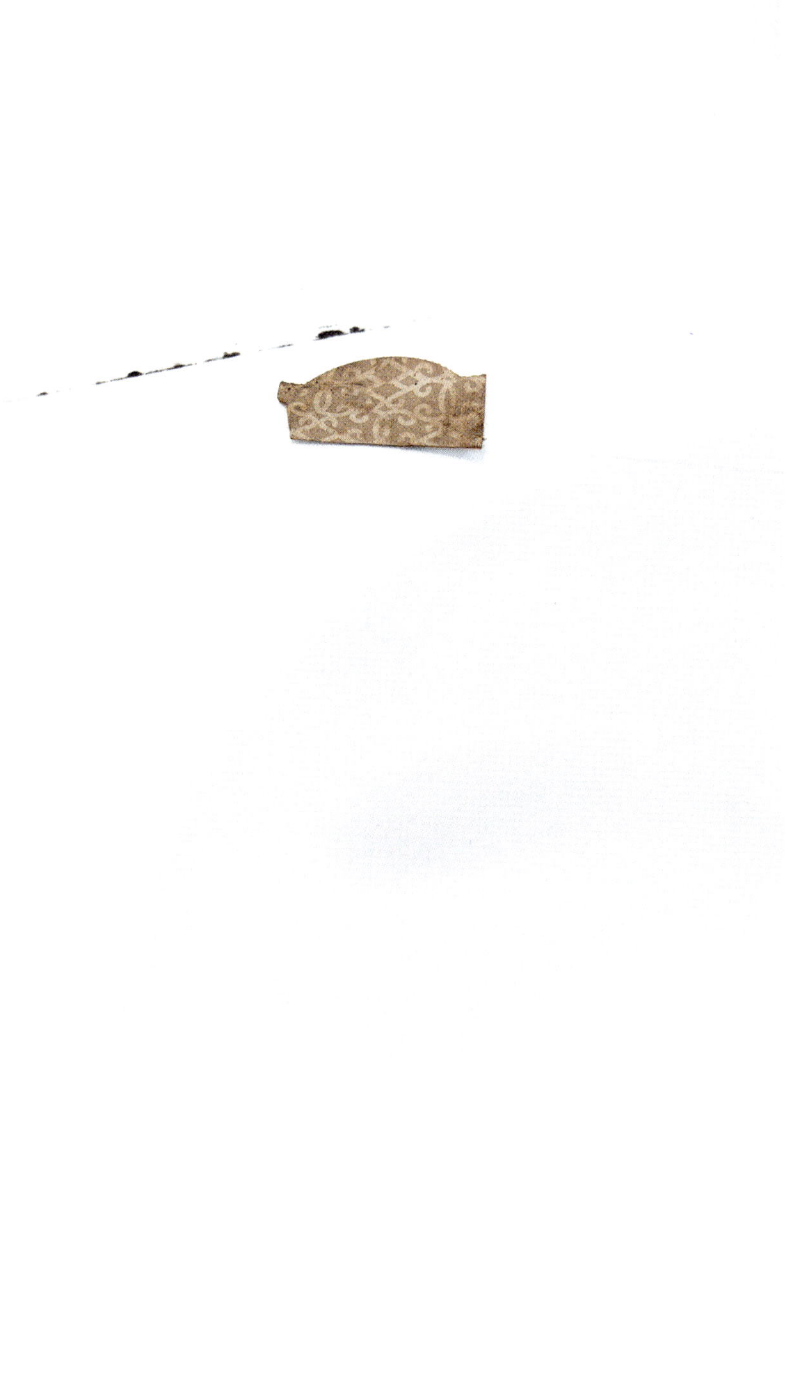

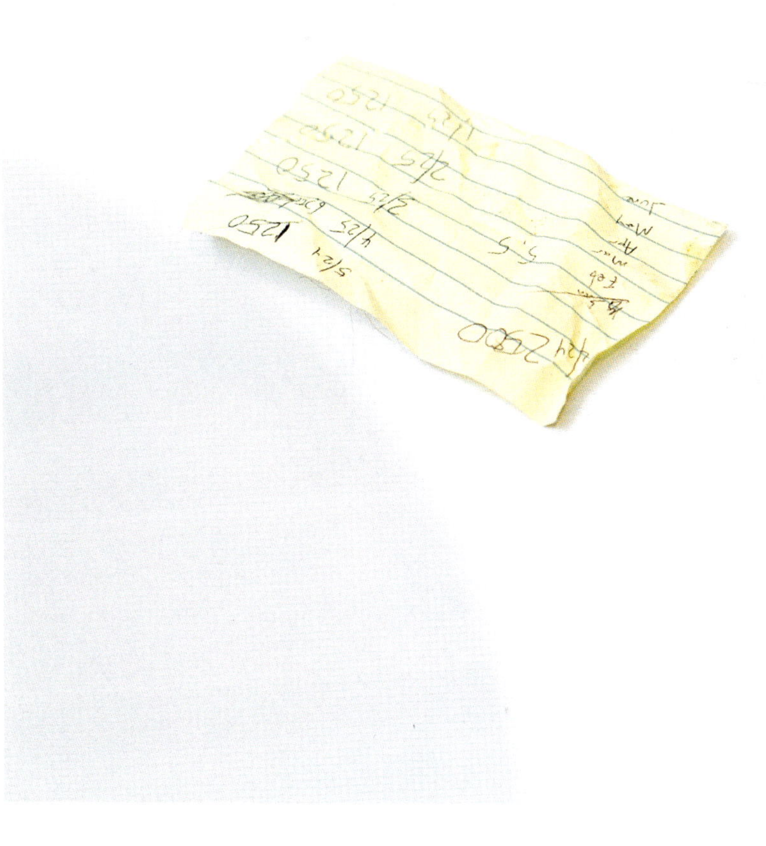

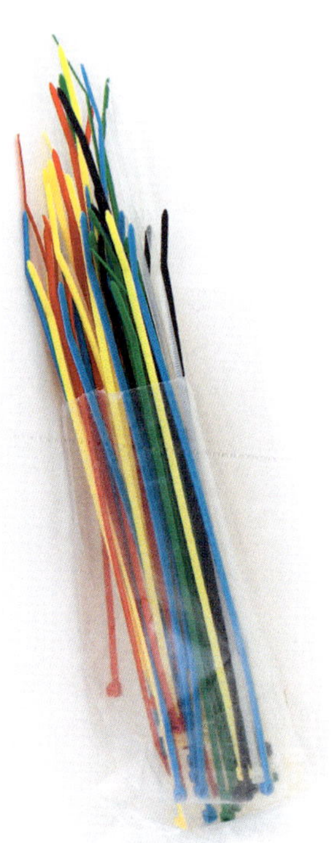

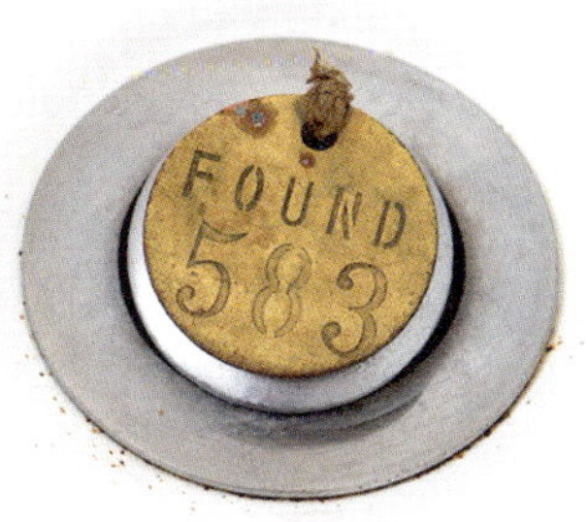
FOUND
583

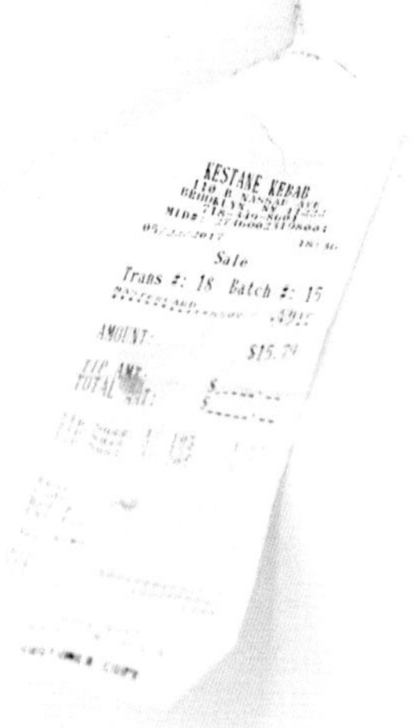

KESTANE KEBAB

Sale

Trans #: 18 Batch #: 15

AMOUNT:

TIP AMT: $

TOTAL AMT: $

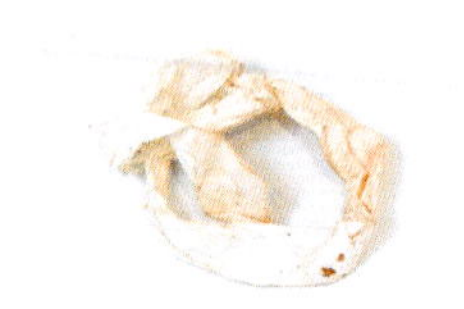

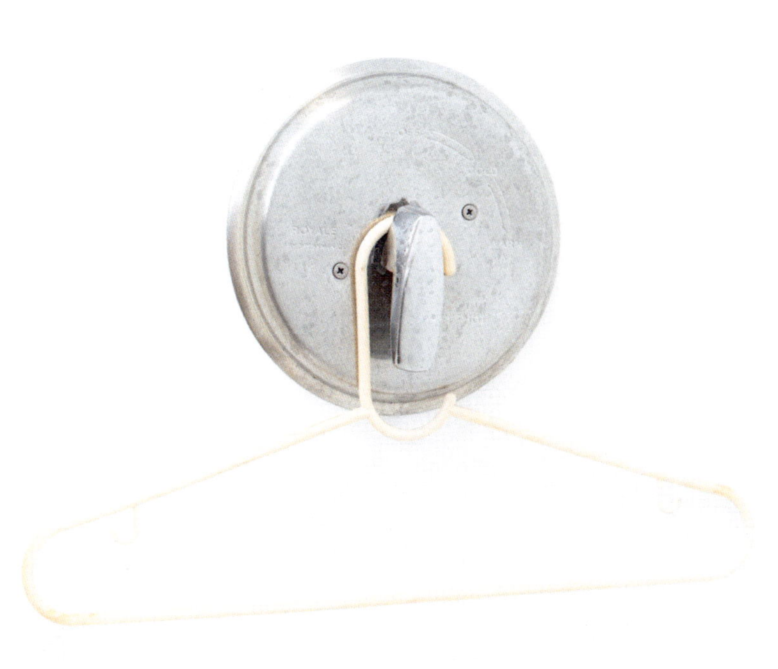

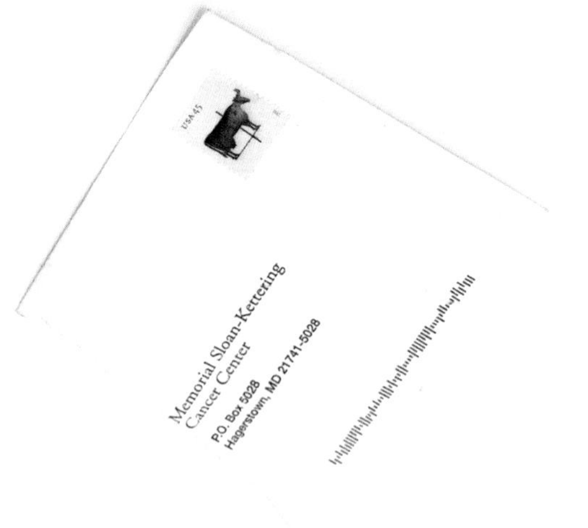
USA 45
Memorial Sloan-Kettering
Cancer Center
P.O. Box 5028
Hagerstown, MD 21741-5028

Jake & Candy
9169192355

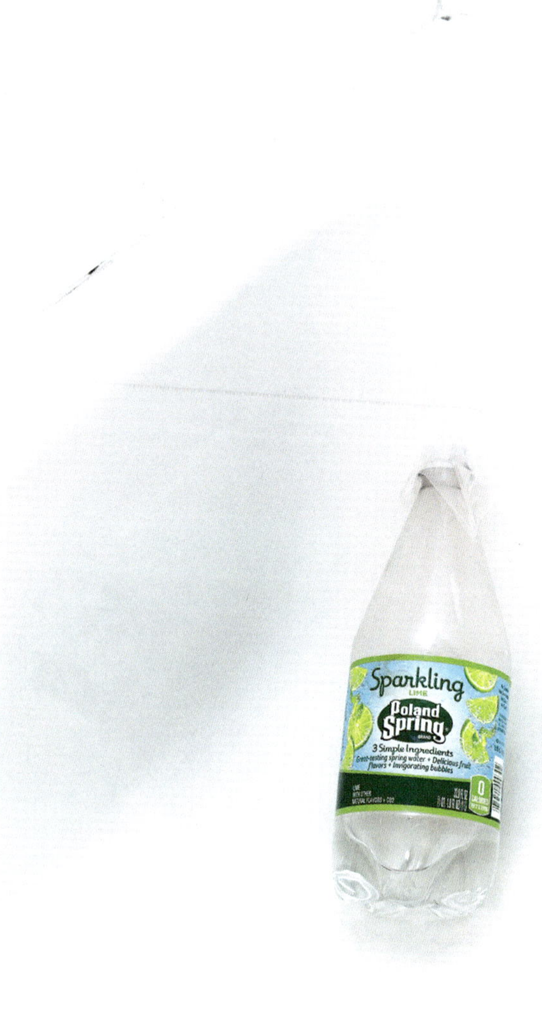

Sparkling
LIME
Poland Spring
3 Simple Ingredients
Great-tasting spring water + Delicious fruit flavors + Invigorating bubbles
0

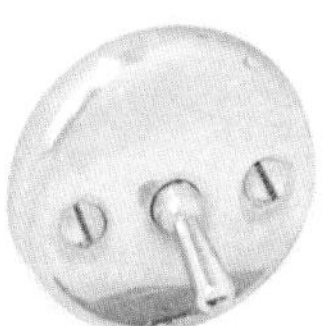

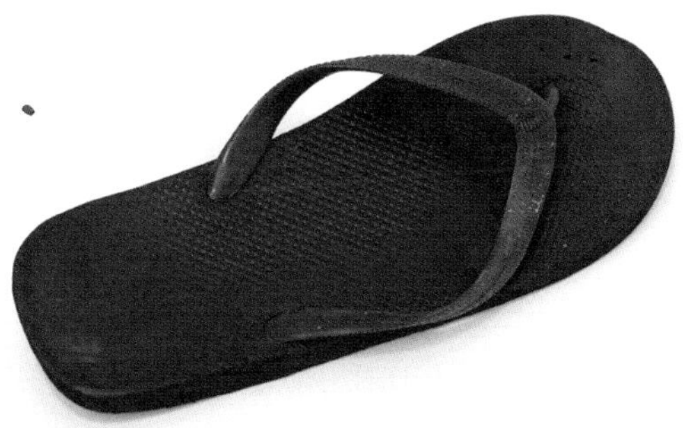

III.

You probably know that expression: "There's always another story."

Matt told me, later, about how the car had gone with him once to an artists' residency—and during a snowstorm was crushed by a falling tree limb. (The limb was later exorcized.)

This anecdote reminded me somehow of my own reasons for being interested in the car, if not its contents, specifically. When I was a child—in that cliché—my parents owned a Volvo that was split in half by a falling tree during a freak tornado that struck western Massachusetts in 1995.

I no longer have access to this car. But I was thinking that somehow I could see its interior, what had happened to it, through Matt's car—never mind that my family's car was a sedan and Matt's an enormous station wagon. I'm not sure if I can tell you what I would have been looking for. So much of my imagination had been used to alter that lost car's interior, to locate faces in its gauges, grates, and dials when I was young.

I have a story that I am constantly trying to tell—and I do admit—I tried to see it in Matt Connors's car.

Also, this isn't even a story, maybe. Really, it isn't a story unless I make it one.

But to proceed more formally:

To the extent that the world is made up of narrative discourse these days, it seems to have two fundamental ingredients or axes: plausibility and syntax. I write, "To the extent..," because I am unsure how great the influence of narrative on current existence really is—or, for that matter, where narrative is. But to the extent that narrative is with us, it seems to manifest itself via *plausibility*, a quality, and *syntax*, a quantity. In other words, narrative has to have some persuasive valence and it has to put things in an order; these are the minimums. We are also apparently living in a time that flatters and elevates the minimum, a curious aesthetic point in itself.

Take, for example, the news, a narrative form. It has lately taken one of the more dramatic turns in our newest era of turns, disruptions, implosions, inflations, and drops. And we could talk, in particular, about a turn, in style and tone, of one of the most-read organs of narrative discourse in the English language, the *New York Times*. Uncertain mental paging backward suggests one signpost of the shift to a buoyant new reportorial voice and enthusiasm for interactive visual media, i.e., video, occurred in mid-2016. The *Times*'s Executive Editor Dean Baquet delivered a memo outlining a coming transformation of the time-honored publication of record, long the haven of "All the News...," etc.

No more would the Gray Lady focus myopically on incremental, event-based coverage; up-to-the-minute announcements, Baquet noted, are available all over the Web. Rather, the *Times* would focus on "authoritative journalism and information readers can use to navigate their lives." Stories would "relax in tone." Editors and reporters would develop pleasing new "story forms" attuned to the continually changing ways in which readers consume information and, I guess, live. Baquet's memo of May 2016 is of a piece with March 2014's Innovation Report, a document that begins with the Sheenian—and now, I suppose, Trumpian—assertion that, "The *New York Times* is winning at journalism." This report admitted the newspaper's urgent need to seduce new readers, along with an ambition to become more "nimble" and fluent in the ways of the digital age. More recently, in January of this year, the 2020 Report appeared. Things look more sanguine (particularly following the so-called Trump-bump of increased subscriptions during the harrowing miasma of post-election days and the interregnum). Baquet's May 2016 memo on the ubiquity of free up-to-the-minute information is expanded, in the 2020 Report, into a thesis about why certain sorts of journalism are less read, "The most poorly read stories, it turns out, are often the most 'dutiful'—incremental pieces, typically with minimal added context, without visuals and largely undifferentiated from the competition. They frequently do not clear the bar of journalism worth paying for, because similar versions are available free elsewhere." The *Times* must now dedicate itself to "All the News That's Worth Paying For," if it is to survive.

To return to my original contention, the *Times* now deals in plausibility, not fact. And it arranges this plausibility, employing a fun, multimedia syntax. These two gestures suffice, at a minimum, to give it a new narrative style. All this is particularly keenly clear to me because, from time to time, I read microfilm versions of the *Times* of yore in the basement of NYU's Bobst Library. I awkwardly manipulate the little film reels and the required viewer for research purposes (this isn't a case of nostalgia!). Although I do not doubt a single one of the eminently reasonable rationales for change supplied in either one of the *Times* reports or the memo above, I've lately been struck, as I scroll through old articles, zooming in and out, by the loss of the former fibrous, drab, newsy tone. On my way home from the library, I'll take a look at the current paper, or, rather, update. My daily *New York Times* "Evening Briefing" appears in my inbox, concluding with a cheery image of some squad of adorable animals or a salute to a counterintuitive and amusing statistic. A sea lion has been rescued in a fuzzy sling! Losing your house keys is, paradoxically, healthful! In spite of myself, I often tremble as I come to the end of the briefing email. I know I'm being courted, entertained, if not pulled back from some imagined psychological brink. In someone's eyes, I may be a bad reader. I may be distracted. I may not know what's going on. And at this moment, as I am reading and recognizing a general plausibility overtaking fact, I often miss that former disregard and professionalism, the hardboiled voice of the mean, old, strict, and somehow trusting paper, the one that talked about "unabashedly savvy real estate" and people who were "stalking a job" (this was the early 2000s, when the table was being set for another implosion), and so on.

If we are readers of realist novels, struggling with the gooey concept of the merely plausible, we might take a long view. We might indulge in some soft epochal categorics. We might say that if the West's nineteenth century was The Century of the Clerk, and the twentieth century The Century of the Teenager, it has already begun to appear, if always prematurely, that the twenty-first century is The Century of the Troll.

Each of the aforementioned figures has its own peculiar relationship to the act of narration. And another obvious tendency allies them: Each labors to reproduce culture. Bartleby, Bob Cratchit, and Bouvard and Pécuchet either did something repetitive or nothing at all; cinema and novels from *The Magic Mountain* to *Lolita*, from *Catcher in the Rye* and *The Bell Jar* to *Infinite Jest*, addressed themselves to individuals on the verge, exploited, ridden with angst, destined to embody whatever culture was, just before they became irrelevant adults; in the contemporary moment, online expressions are relentlessly repeated, dissected, distorted, redistributed, but are there any good novels about this yet? Or is it that everything now is about this, including elections? We know well the clerk's superannuated affect, either nonexistent or mystifyingly attuned to minutiae. The teenager longs, weeps, rages, and ironizes, as the curtain of the most American of centuries falls on a pharmacologically managed excess of anxiety and deficit of attention. And now we seem to wonder if we should bother awakening into the next hundred years (How much further will human consciousness—not to speak of earnest emotion—make it?).

The troll, broadly defined, is not a critic or satirist, so much as a weird method actor. The troll has traditionally participated by defining participation itself in an ambiguous if not absolutely negative light. The troll establishes the terms of others' commitment to truth (which is to say, to any idealized and apparently unmediated entity) and reflects these back as image and/or text, and incessantly. But the troll's either antisocial or paradoxically altruistic (or, both) interventions have already been extensively analyzed by individuals more qualified than I, and I would merely like to draw from this somewhat hastily defined category a general sense of why the plausible is so important—and how we can possibly give this category a more active, if not positive, valence.

Looking into a series of fragments I've jotted down in a notebook, I come across the following vague question, "Given the variety of temporalities that exist, solutions?" I've also written a phrase, "Lack of a preexisting commons." And another strange question, "Does what we cannot forget take the form of an event?" In my own thinking around narrative, I'm familiar with discontinuity. It's taken me years to learn to write a legible paragraph, and I still approach prose with trepidation, as it's a highly artificial undertaking for me. (The way I think feels nothing like what I am doing here.) All the same, I am interested in the aspects of narrative that occur at the intersection of technique and reflection, and in prose, though of course not all narration occurs in prose. Plausibility probably seems, at face value, like an extremely, even depressingly, insignificant quality of narrative. Indeed, it is. But plausibility, as a mere or minor way of addressing what is the case, of softening the copula from fast equivalency to meandering dotted line, offers us something by way of method that should not be ignored. Much as the troll proceeds from categories in which truth and the sublime are not merely under erasure but the tortured disillusionment leading to said erasure itself constitutes a risible piety, those who manipulate the plausible begin from an analogous point of liberty—a liberty that may also double as disaffection, alienation, boredom, despair. Yet those who play upon plausibility rather than actuality rescue contemplation from foolhardy ideals as well as from paranoid excoriation and embarrassingly principled condemnation. Or, rather, in the weird light of the subjunctive, such writers might, under the right conditions, permit contemplation to occur. (Plausibility need not, for example, be a species of pandering. . . .)

Are these writings a poetic text on these terms? A tissue of citations? Of indexes? Yes, there are any number of indexes offered up here, indeed I have found "things," but what I am interested in is not what they prove about a continuous contemporary space, a "past" flat and plausibly real, but what their superimposition (collage-style) atop one another can say, as we build it toward our present. These items (from the car) were never, I would contend, part of a clearly continuous space and time. How would I establish, anyway, their proper, exact, correct distance or proximity to one another?

A weird thing to ask: *Was* the car static? Is it? And: Where are its limits?

Matt says to me, "I am documenting these objects that everyone else seems to have so much more interest in than I have apparently had for the last several years."

141

I want to observe that I've seen two sides of Matt in the process of working on this: One, by way of which he claims that the project of cataloguing the car was a way of stepping aside, of avoiding agency while still participating, contributing to some sort of collaborative undertaking. Another in which the descriptive work

I have done on his car and the objects inside it begins to seem like a plot against him.

"Why are you recording this?" he'd say, as I made a recording of him talking to me about the car and then, somehow, also his life (it got mixed into things, unavoidably). "Is this the interview happening now? Are you going to transcribe this?"

I listen to my own voice in the two recordings I made of us discussing the car and the cataloguing project. The first conversation was conducted in a cement-block dorm room at Ithaca College while Matt made photographs of stuff from the car in his bathtub, in June of 2017 (I lay on the floor in the other room); the second took place in a garden near the offices of a program I teach in at NYU, in May of 2018.

When I listen to myself in these two recordings I think: I sound harsh, green. I laugh from time to time, as if there truly is some sort of structure here, as if I know what I'm doing. And: As if it's funny that Matt might wish to renounce his connection to the car and the things in it—or, on the other hand, and maybe relatedly, suspect me of attempting to entrap him.

Because he's the one who originally proposed this.

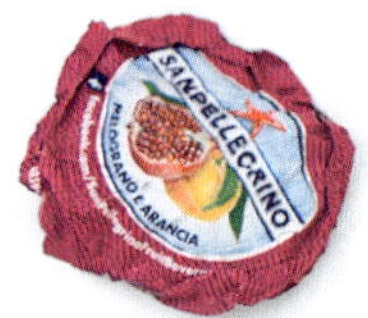
SANPELLEGRINO
MELOGRANO E ARANCIA

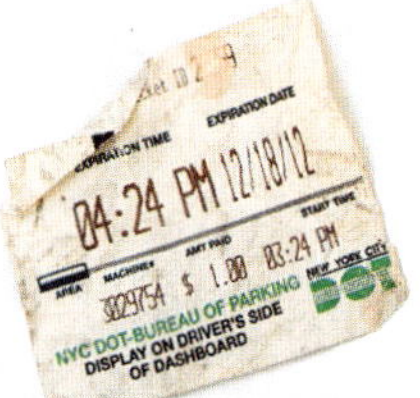
EXPIRATION TIME
EXPIRATION DATE
04:24 PM 12/18/12
AREA
MACHINE#
AMT PAID
START TIME
3029754 $ 1.00 03:24 PM
NEW YORK CITY
DOT
NYC DOT-BUREAU OF PARKING
DISPLAY ON DRIVER'S SIDE
OF DASHBOARD

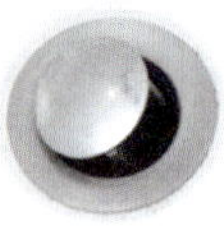

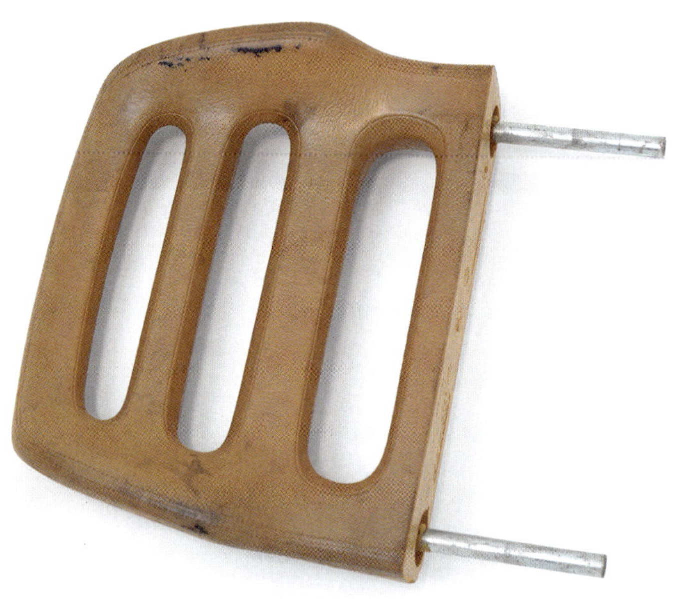

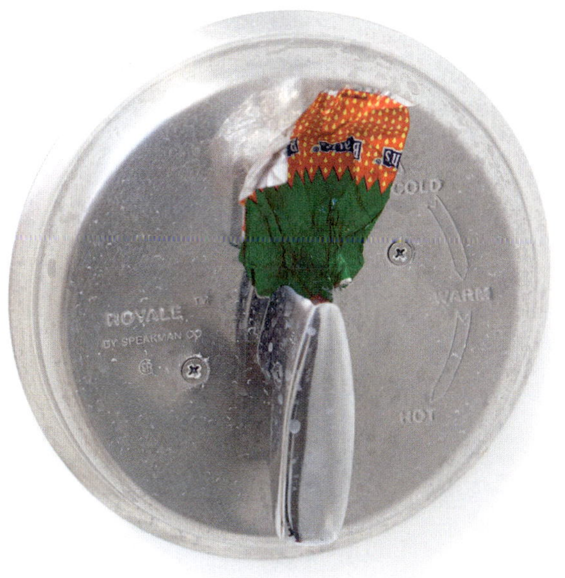
ROYALE
BY SPEARMAN CO
COLD
WARM
HOT

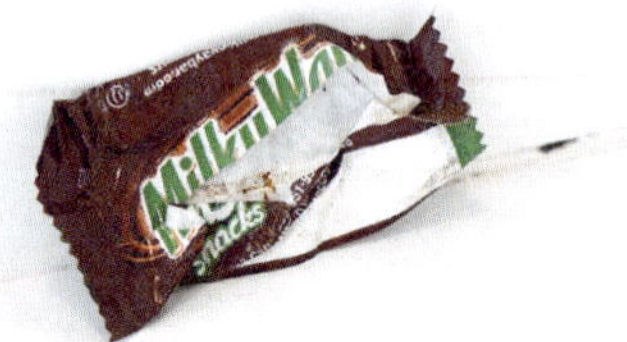

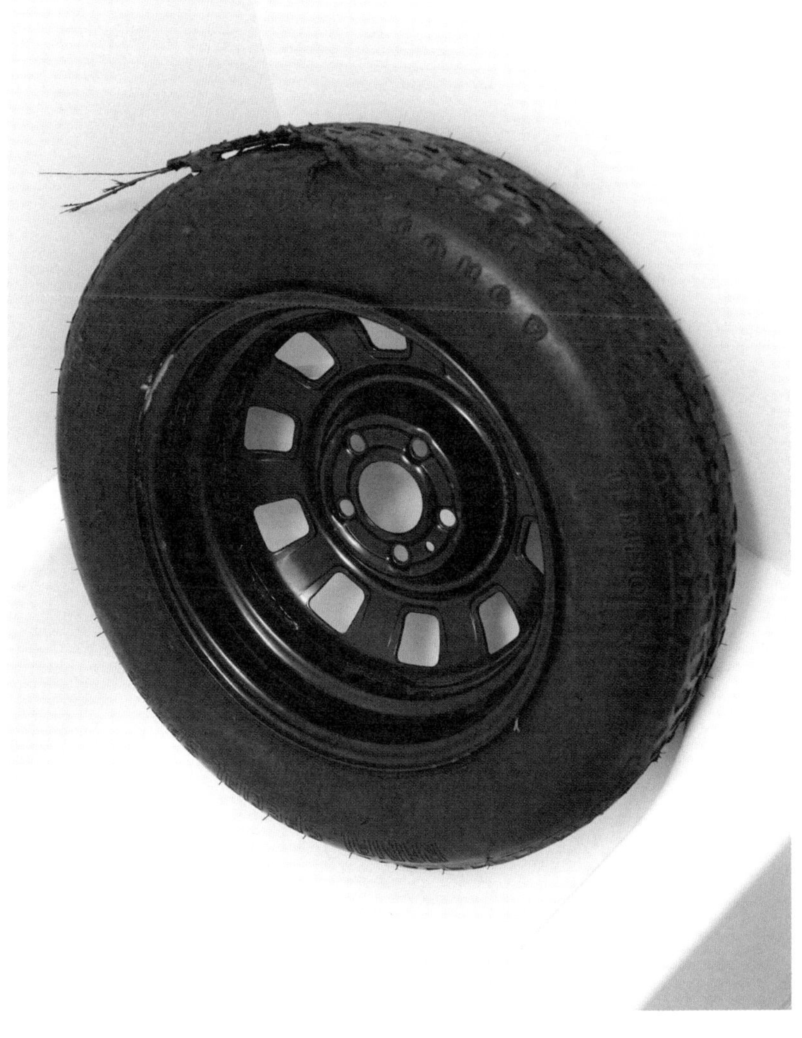

CONNORS,MATTHEW,C
880 LORIMER ST AP 2R
BROOKLYN NY 11222

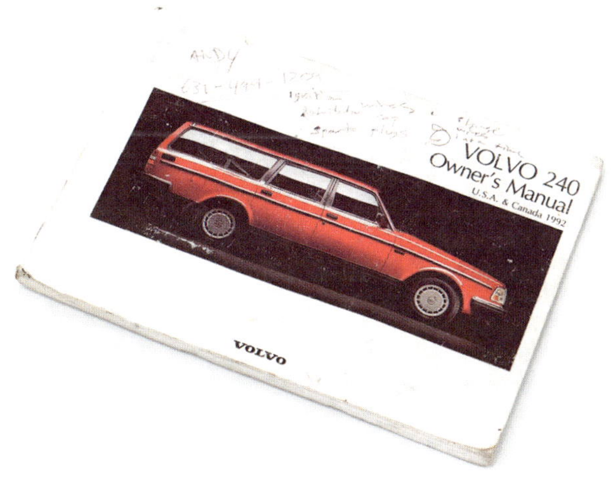
VOLVO 240
Owner's Manual
U.S.A. & Canada 1992
VOLVO

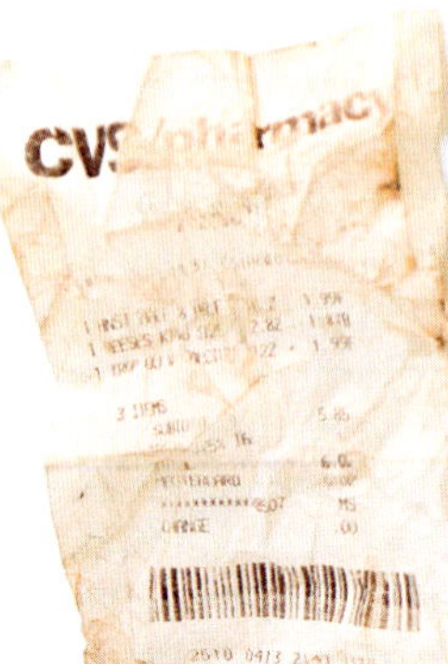
CVS
GET YOUR CVS EXTRACARE

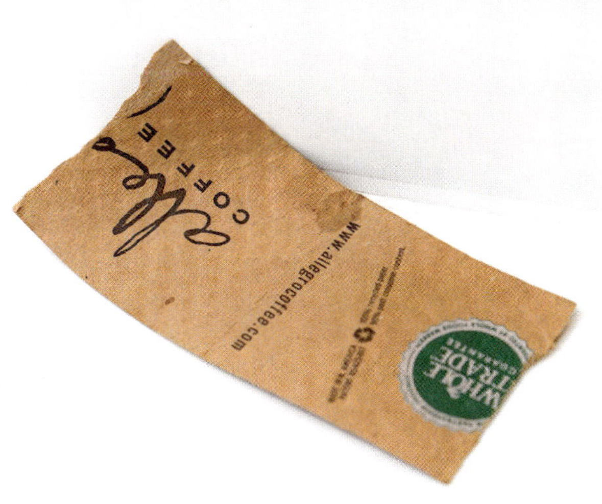
COFFEE
www.allegrocoffee.com
WHOLE TRADE

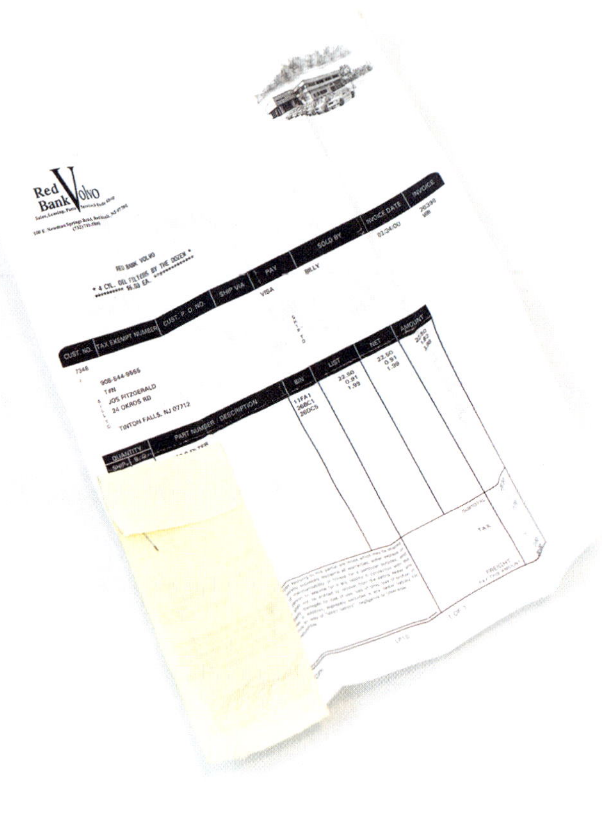

Red Bank Volvo

100 E. Newman Springs Road, Red Bank, NJ 07701

RED BANK VOLVO

* 4 CYL. OIL FILTERS BY THE DOZEN *

CUST. NO.	TAX EXEMPT NUMBER	CUST. P. O. NO.	SHIP VIA	PAY	SOLD BY	INVOICE DATE	INVOICE
7348				VISA	BILLY	03/24/00	26396

908-544-9555
T#N
JOS FITZGERALD
24 OKROS RD
TINTON FALLS, NJ 07712

QUANTITY SHIP	B.O.	PART NUMBER / DESCRIPTION	BIN	LIST	NET	AMOUNT
			11FA1	22.50	22.50	
			26BC1	0.91	0.91	
			26DC5	1.99	1.99	

SUBTOTAL
TAX
FREIGHT

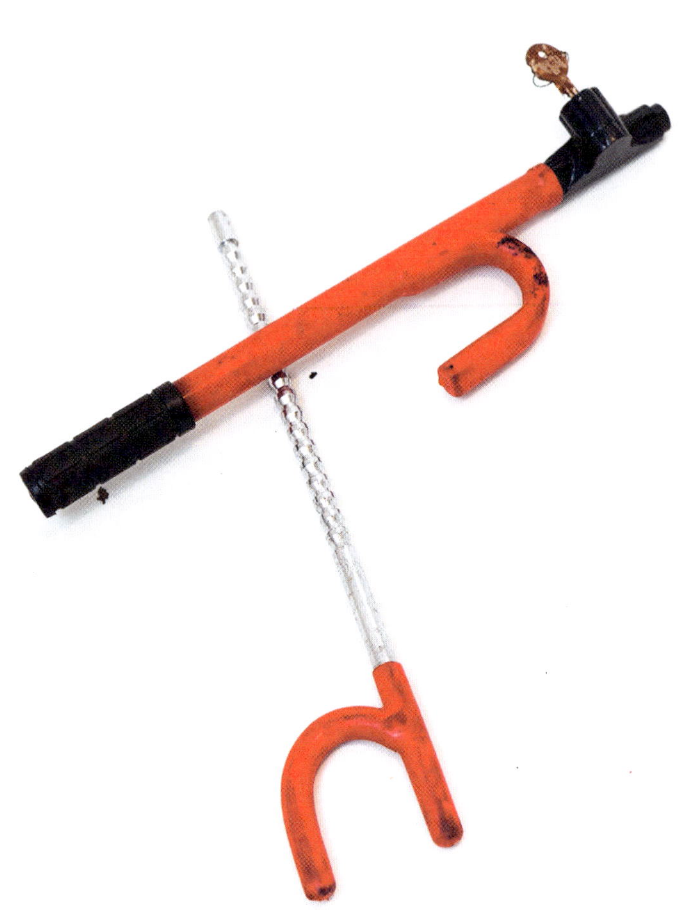

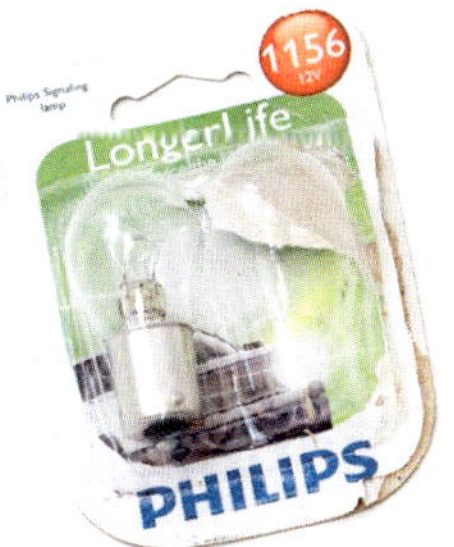
1156
12V
Philips Signaling
lamp
LongerLife
PHILIPS

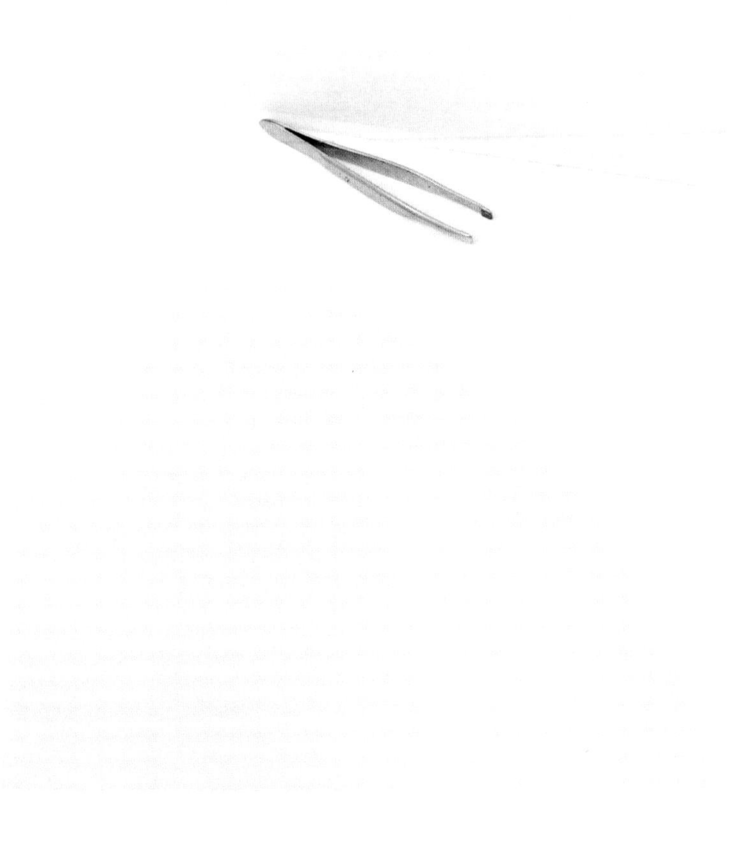

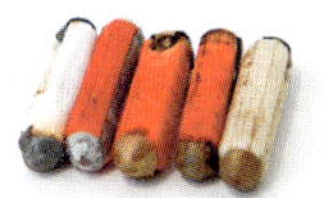

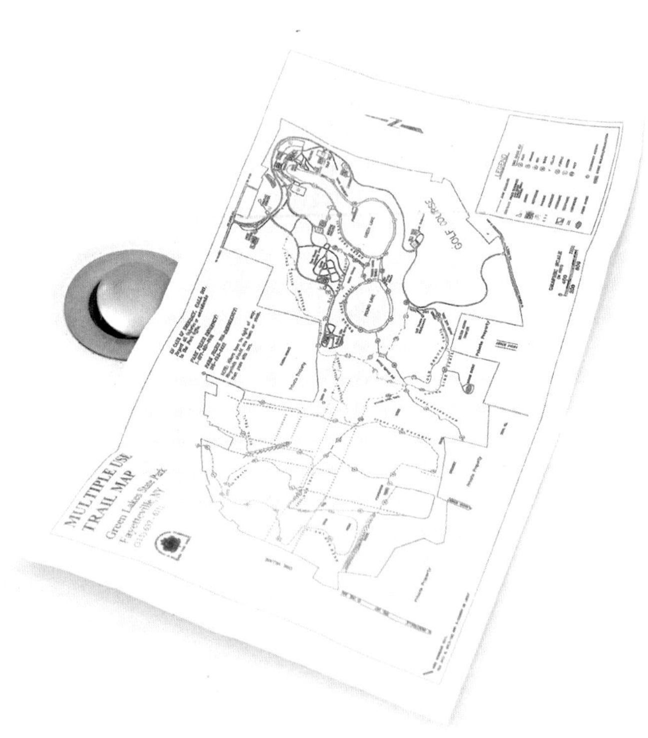

MULTIPLE USE
TRAIL MAP
Green Lakes State Park
Fayetteville, NY
GOLF COURSE
LEGEND

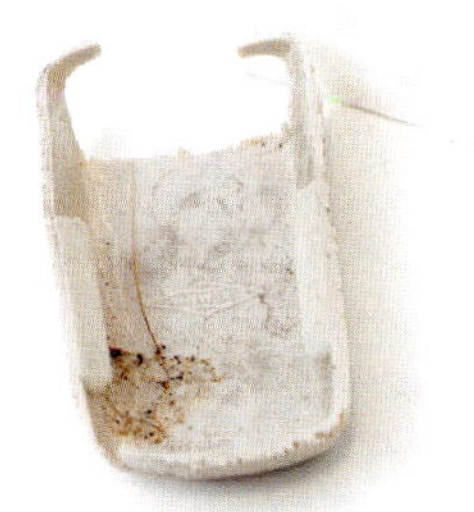

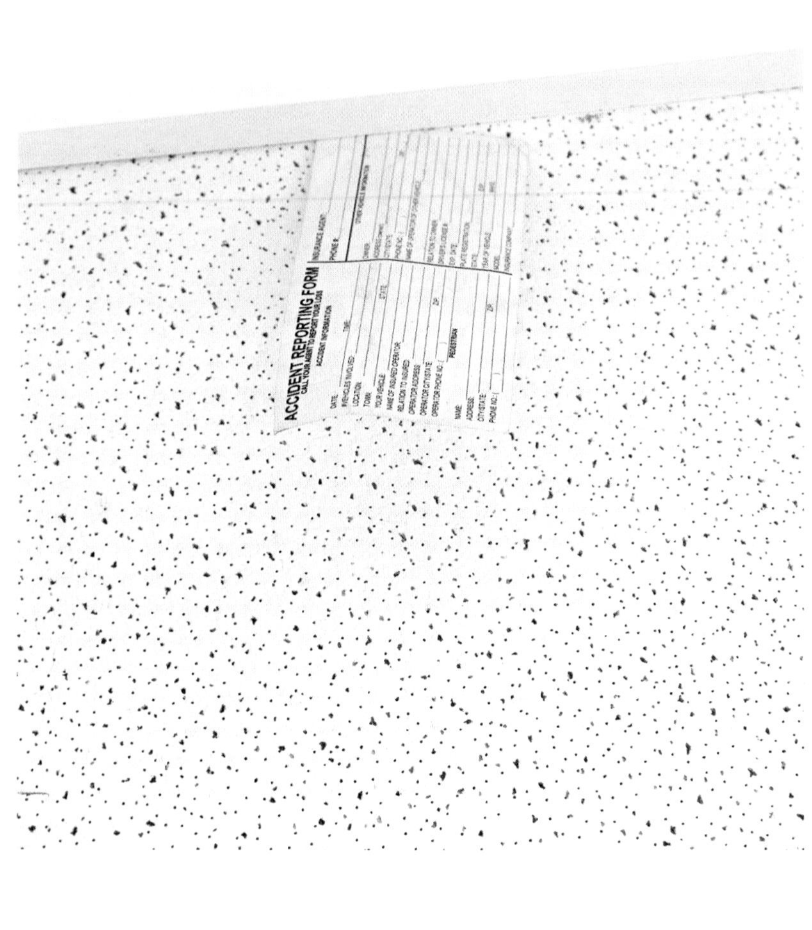
ACCIDENT REPORTING FORM
CALL YOUR AGENT TO REPORT YOUR LOSS
ACCIDENT INFORMATION
PEDESTRIAN

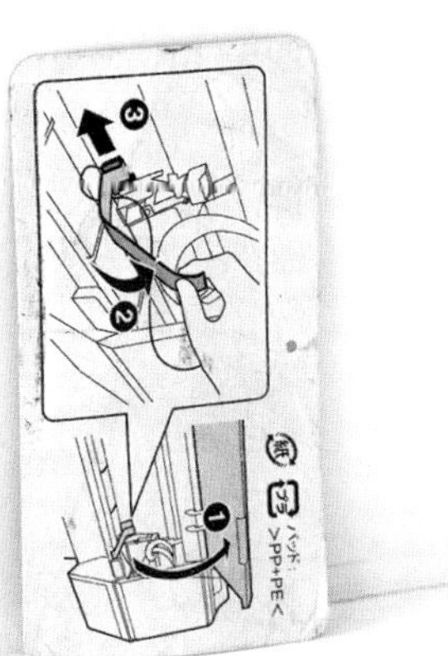
紙
プラ
パッド：
>PP+PE<

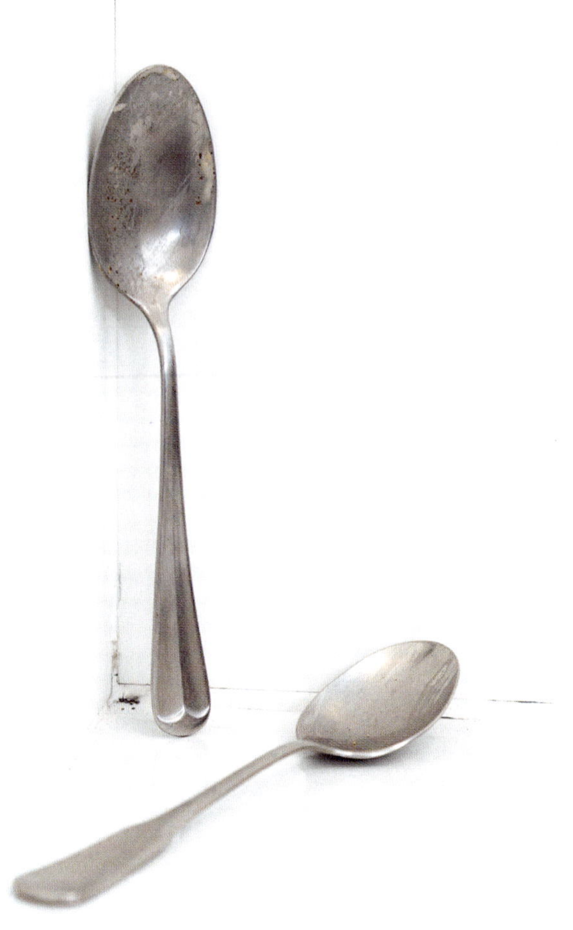

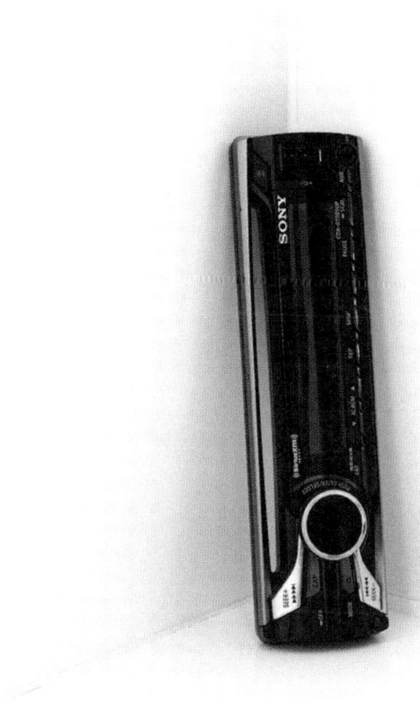
SONY

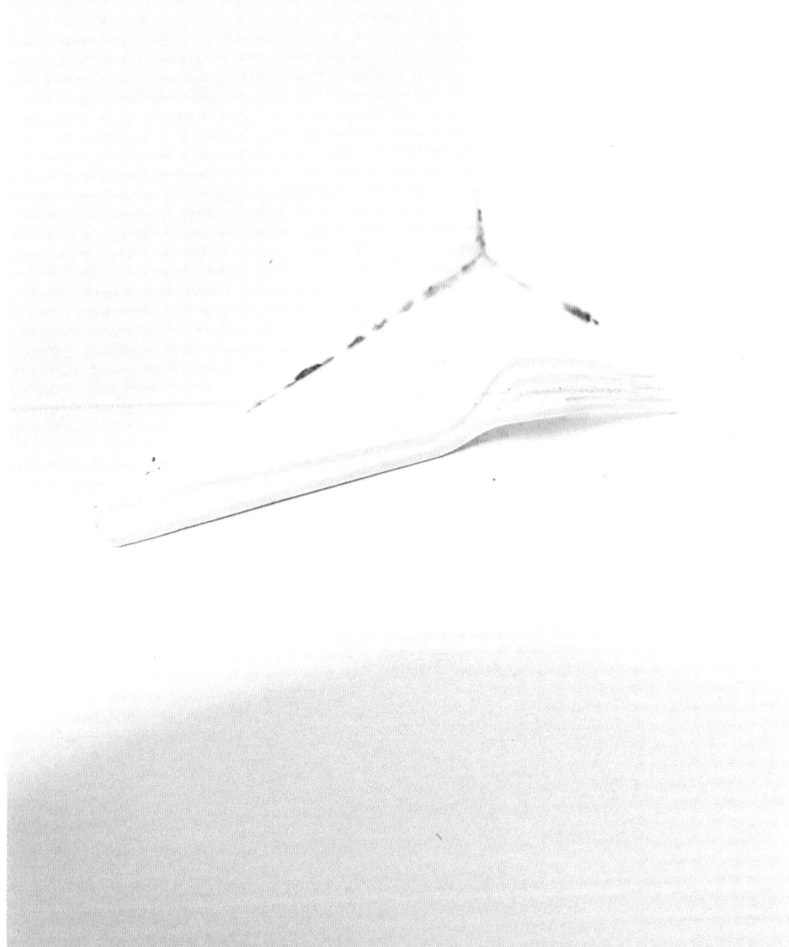

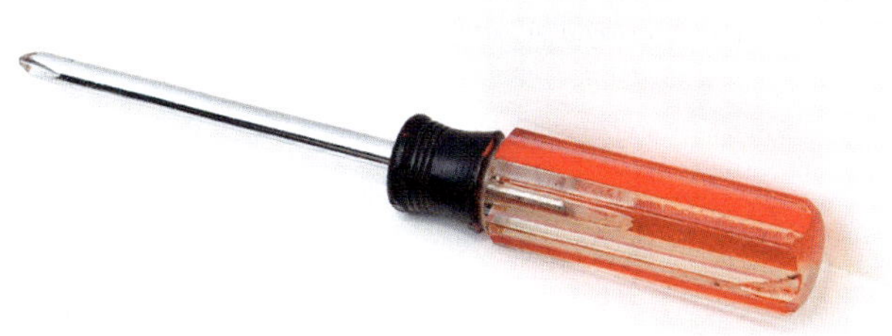

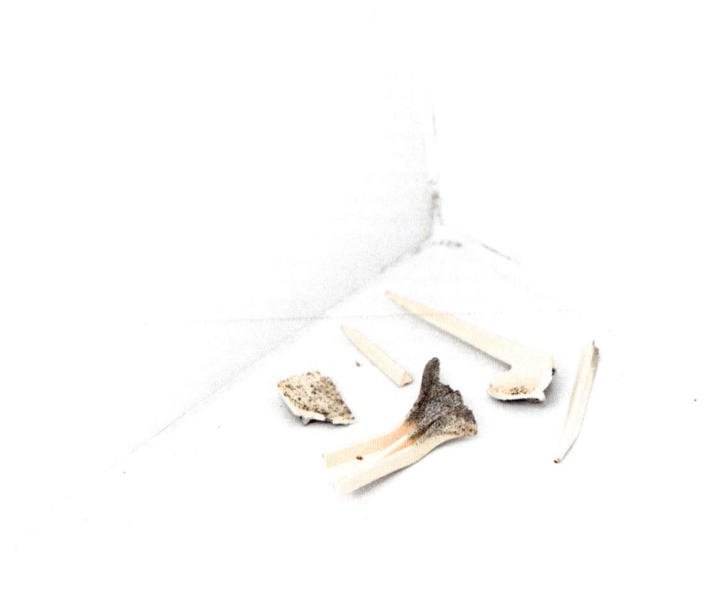

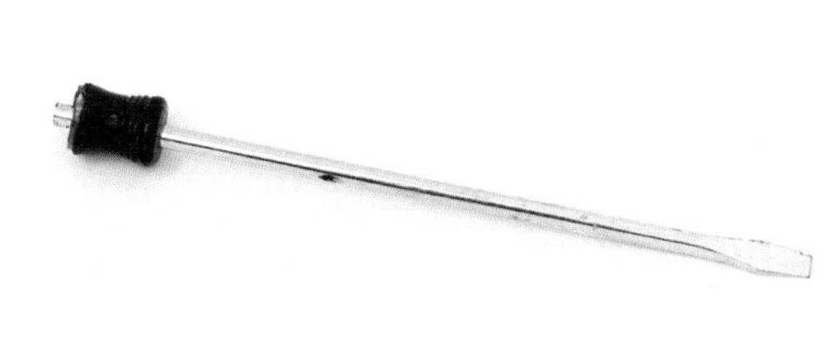

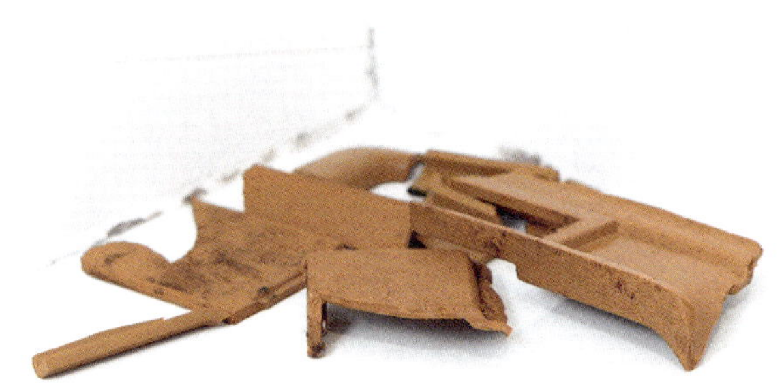

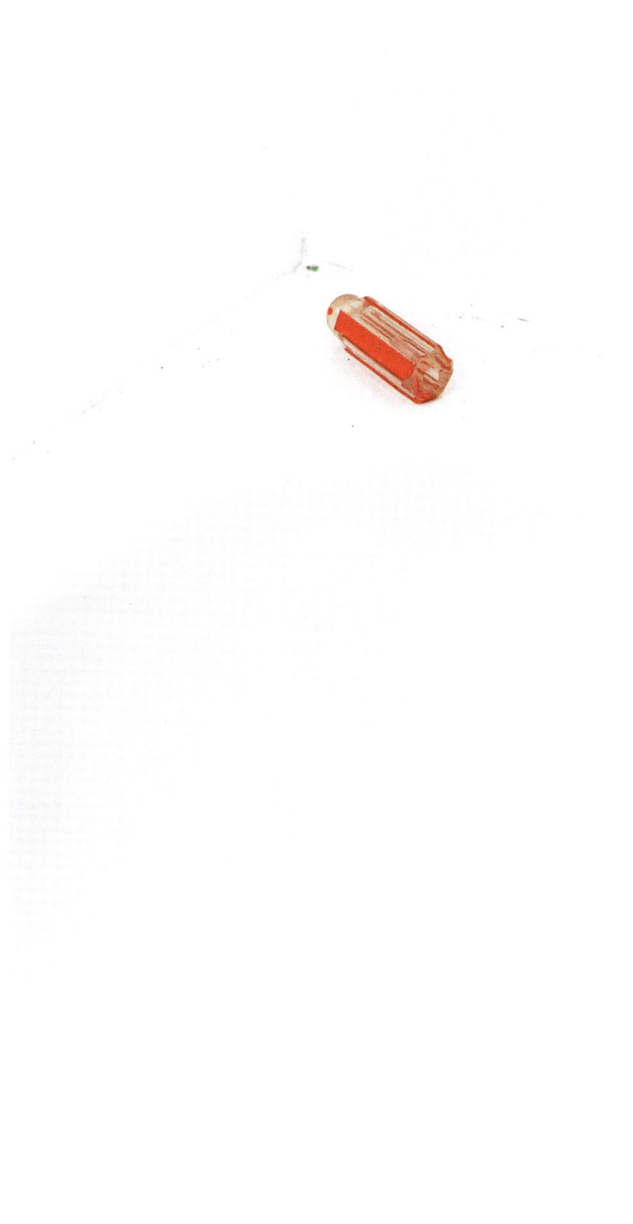

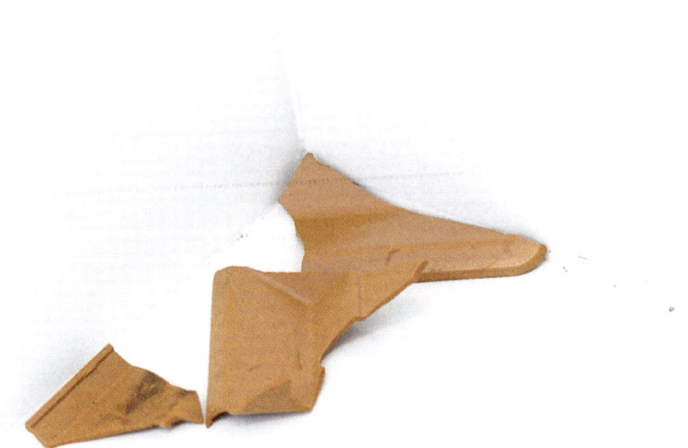

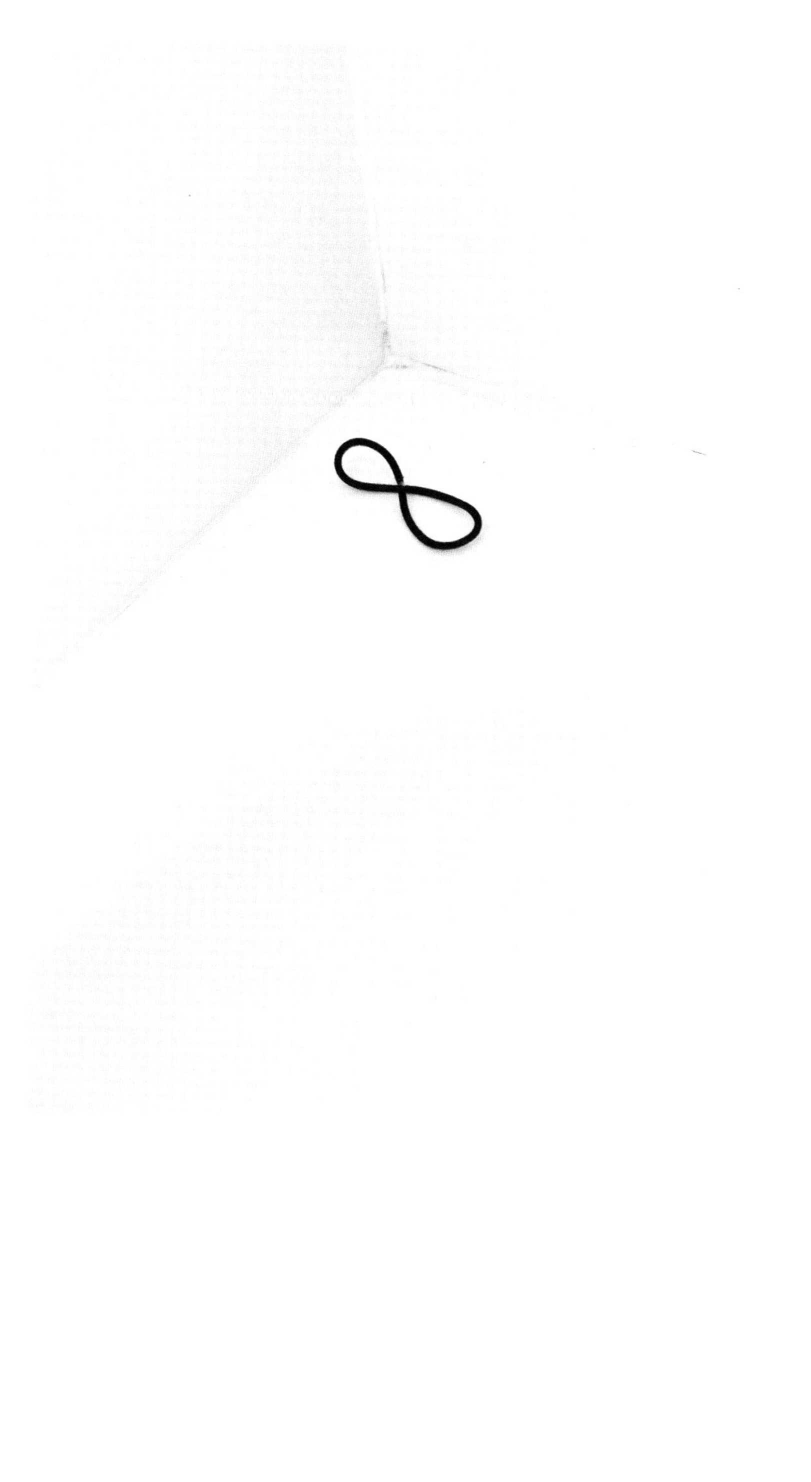

IV.

I used to have a photograph of that car from my childhood, after it was split in half. The car was beige and the photograph was blurry, as if it had been taken by accident. But it's likely I lost even that. I think it's likely that I knew, even in that summer of two years ago, when we catalogued the contents of Matt's car, that I was in the process of losing something I would be unlikely to regain. Of course, the vast majority of the things we lose do not come back to us.

Here is what Aristotle has to say: He says that the key mechanism is recognition. Now, that's a murky and maybe even dangerous formulation—and people have had various problems with it. But he also says that he doesn't completely or exhaustively know what the object of recognition could or should be. He says something disparaging about inanimate objects but not much more.

What if the object of recognition is the whole book? What if the hero of the story, the one upon whose recognition the plot/narrative turns, is the reader herself?

I am willing to admit that it would not be inaccurate to say that I write with a mirror in hand. But in fact there is no mirror. A phantom or unreal version of the vaudeville marksman, or *woman*, I appear to look away from what I am aiming at, what I apparently seek to describe. When I write I employ a system of mirrors. It is not that they are real mirrors, that you would ever be able to see them in real life. But they entrap images of the world, all the same. This is the sort of appliance fiction is for me: I use it to look away from something and still perceive it. I can speak—and, write—about a thing that has been placed directly behind my head. I adjust various reflective surfaces accordingly. They tremble at the ends of wands; the joints are slightly loose; it takes some patience. A scene comes into view.

Everything I've just said is metaphor, of course, but it's one of the best ways I've come up with for describing what it is I want to do with fiction, by which I mean, *with prose*. My mirror is imperfect and provisional, as all metaphors are, and I don't yet fully understand it. Elsewhere, I've called fiction a device for "seeing around corners." I recently told someone, "Fiction is a way of seeing around corners. It's a system of mirrors that isn't designed to catch my own image, but rather images of what I'm not able or permitted to see in my actual life. I'm not exactly sure how it is you can know something that you don't know, but fiction works like that for me. It's a device for collecting information." I think when I said this I was thinking of an image of a periscope I once saw advertised in the back of a children's magazine—but a text is slightly different from a set of carefully aligned mirrors and you have to look into it at least twice to see the kind of image I'm talking about. You aren't looking at reality; it's hard not to look at reality but you have to recognize this and you have to wait until you see the contours of another thing, which is in fact the thing. In fiction, the thing itself is always something that you could not see in life, so called. This, for me, is the definition of fiction, where it is and how it happens. And in this sense, fiction is not merely or exclusively about "making things up." But it isn't not about making things up, either.

Thus the comparative nature of this project, this essay, also constitutes its unreality, its fictive aspect. I am not exactly or always telling stories; I tell superimpositions, overlaps, coincidences, delays. This is my thinking, not diegesis but: recurrence, a style of conjunction, an elevation of what remains unfinished.

We can only determine how things look if we see them *through* one another.

One last thing here: Perhaps you are wondering if we found something in the car. And that's what I am trying to tell you, that of course we did.

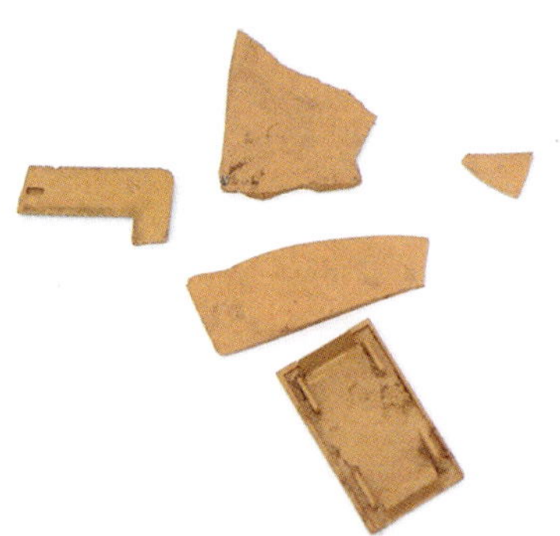

Acknowledgments

Lucy and Matt would like to thank the students and instructors of Image Text Ithaca, summer 2017, for their kind participation in this project. These brilliant individuals include: masterminds Catherine Taylor and Nicholas Muellner, Stanley Wolukau-Wanambwa, Claudia Rankine, Matthew Baczewski, Edith Fikes, Pablo Lerma, Martha Ormiston, Guy Pettit, Janet Solval, and Grant Willing.

The images in this book benefited considerably from the technical prowess of Campbell Silverstein, Stefan Bottomley, Harry's Auto Repair, Knight's Autobody, Shade Tree Auto, and Moe.

Lucy and Matt would also like to thank Elana Schlenker for her amazing design and offer their reverence for her equanimity in the face of bedbugs.

Some fragments of Lucy's essay were originally published by the Poetry Foundation; thanks, as ever, to Michael Slosek. An interview with Tan Lin, first published in *Bomb*, also furnishes a short passage; thank you, Tan, for the conversation and for your writing. The title of the essay by Sara Ahmed quoted is "Creating disturbance: Feminism, happiness, and affective difference." A salute of gratitude to the anonymous email writer (that was a fantastic email). And, last but not least, Lucy wishes to thank Matthew Connors for his extraordinary generosity.

The Poetics

Design by Studio Elana Schlenker
Printed in Lithuania by Kopa in an edition of 500

First printing

ISBN: 978-0-9967351-8-6

Image Text Ithaca Press
Nicholas Muellner and Catherine Taylor, Editors
Image Text Ithaca is an initiative of Ithaca College

imagetextithaca.com